An illustrated history of

'THE BIG HOUSE'

Arlebury Park House & Estate since the 1770s

New Alresford, Hampshire, England

The history of the estate exemplifies much of the huge social and economic change that took place during the 18th through to the 21st centuries.

This history is about the owners of the Arlebury estate and how it was developed over nearly 250 years. It is also about the times they lived in, how they influenced the town of New Alresford and its surroundings, and how the changing wider world affected them.

2019

© Jan Field

Arlebury is a private residence not open to the public but is an important part of our local heritage. All proceeds from the sale of this work go to the Alresford Society.

<u>*For further information about the Society visit*</u> *www.thealresfordsociety.co.uk*

Or contact: Jan Field, Chairman, The Alresford Society

email jan@alresford.f9.co.uk

3 Arlebury Park Mews, Alresford, SO24 9ER

A SOCIAL & ECONOMIC HISTORY OF ARLEBURY

CONTENTS   PAGE

FIGURES

APPENDICES

Acknowledgements

Two local historians, Brian Rothwell and Peter Pooley, helped to get me started on what turned out to be a long journey of exploration! Brian wrote a lovely book *'The Streams of the Itchen'*[1] , that includes brief references to Arlebury but little detail, so this history is intended to fill a gap. Peter Pooley proposed further development of the themes of social and economic change in the 18th to 21st centuries - a quarter of a millennium. The history of the estate exemplifies much of this change.

Rosemary Chambers book *'True to My Roots'*[2], includes coverage of Old Alresford House, where she was born. Her parents had considered Arlebury when looking for a country house away from the approaching war-time bombs in the late 1930s but chose Old Alresford House instead. Helping edit her book spurred me on to find out more about Arlebury.

The excellent Hampshire Record Office in Winchester has been a fascinating source of maps, wills, drawings, photographs, books and more, and archivist David Rymill helped to interpret arcane documents. The British Newspaper Archives are also an excellent source of records in local papers. Churches are also a time-honoured source of information and both St John's, Alresford and St Andrew's, Tichborne, contain memorials to the Harris, Marx and Walford families who were the main occupants of Arlebury in its heyday as a private residence, from the late 1770s until nearly the end of WW2.

Descendants of families can be a primary source of information but all five children of William and Jenny Harris (the founders) died before them. Andrew Marx had begun a history of his family's ownership of the estate from the mid-19th century but sadly he died in January 2014 before completing his task. My thanks to him, though, for information provided when he visited Alresford in 2013 and for some interesting emails. There is a history of the Walford family on the internet, including mention of Arlebury, and its author, John Walford, kindly provided more recent information as well.

Ernie Witchard bought Arlebury in 1944 from the Walfords, converting the house into 8 large flats but sold in 1949 to Sidney Martin, who sold it back to the Witchard family in 1976/7. Their children, Jim Witchard and Elizabeth Martin, who knew each other all their lives, each kindly contributed many memories of Arlebury. Sadly, Jim died in 2016 and his wife Mary the year before but Elizabeth Martin lives in the West Lodge in Drove Lane, which her father Sidney moved into when he sold 'the Big House'. Residents in Arlebury Park House, The Mews and The Barns also kindly provided memories and photos

Most of the newer, colour photographs are my own but the Hampshire Record Office, New Alresford Town Trust and John Walford have kindly provided others. Godfrey Andrews, keeper of Alresford Heritage, has provided several taken in the early 1900s, which he has cleaned and restored.

Finally, thanks to the Society's Committee members for their encouragement.

The problem with research is that the more you do, the more you realise you could still do … but I must stop somewhere. This history may stir other memories amongst residents of Alresford and perhaps there will be an update in due course.   *Jan Field*

---

[1] 'The Streams of the Itchen', Sue & Brian Rothwell, Alresford Literary & Historical Society, 2014.
[2] 'True to My Roots', Rosemary Chambers, Lake House, The Soke, Alresford, 2014.

Figure 1 –Aerial view of Arlebury Park Estate - Listed in Hampshire's 'Historic Parks & Gardens'[3]

Photograph © 2016 Google & © 2016 Infoterra Ltd. & Bluesky

The Arlebury estate dates from the last quarter of the 18th century. This history began life as a means of recording and protecting an important piece of Alresford's heritage, surprisingly little documented previously, perhaps because although described as an important part of the town's character[3] it is outside the designated conservation area, the focus of most local histories. A record has, therefore, been submitted to Hampshire's Archaeology & Historic Buildings Record and to Winchester City Council's Historic Environment Record as a key part of Alresford's identity, helping to give the town its 'sense of place' and its 'local distinctiveness'. As such, it has protection under the National Planning Policy Framework, 'Conserving and enhancing the Historic Environment' and Historic England's guidance on protecting heritage assets, rural landscapes and Historic Environment Records. Included in the Hampshire Register of Historic Parks & Gardens[4], Arlebury also sits in an Area of Special Landscape Quality and is bordered on the north by the River Itchen, locally called the Arle. It is one of England's world-famous chalk streams and a Hampshire & Isle of Wight Wildlife Trust 'Living Landscape' (Appendix 1), including SAC, SINC & SSSI designations.

Despite these protections, a development company that owned the field just a hundred yards in front of

---

[3] Winchester City Council Character Assessment 2004. *'A large proportion of parks were created in the eighteenth century, when the construction of large country houses was associated with a designed landscape setting. These are generally located on lower ground and valley sides and can be associated with settlements. Typical examples include Ovington House and Park,* **Arlebury Park***, Northington Grange, Old Alresford House, Lainston House, Tichbourne Park and Warnford Park'.*

[4] The defined area of the Hampshire listed park & garden runs from Drove Lane to the western edge of the Recreation Ground, on the far right of this photograph. The Historic Environment Record (Winchester City Council, p.41) also records this. There is, though, a good case to be made that the listing should extend to The Dean.

1

the 'Big House' (Figure 1 above and front cover), proposed building some 30 houses here. Realistically, it was unlikely to be given planning permission but residents of the house and mews cottages alongside formed a consortium and bought the field - just in case! Since then, part of the field to the right of Figure 1, fronting The Avenue and part of the estate for centuries, has also been under threat of devastating intrusion into this special landscape. Planning permission has been refused more than once but we have to stay vigilant!

Arlebury (initially called 'New Place') has a good story to tell in its own right. Since Georgian times, this was 'the Big House' in Alresford. The Oxford English Dictionary defines this as '... the largest house in a village or area, typically inhabited by a family of high social standing'. This was certainly the case in the 18th century when it was built, and even in Peter Campion's 1922 book 'A recent history of Hampshire'[5], Arlebury was still a private residence, noted as one of the 'Principal Seats in Hampshire', alongside Old Alresford House, Ropley Manor and others.

The house itself and surrounding parkland and gardens have been significantly altered over the years by the successive owners. The *original* house, dating from the late 1770s/1780s was a handsome, albeit *relatively* modest example of a Georgian-style country property but, although later extensions faithfully retained much of the Georgian style, they were actually added during the Victorian era. The garden and 'home park' have also changed over the years but still include a number of splendid veteran trees, including exotic Cedars of Lebanon and native lime trees, now between 150 and 200 years old.

To begin this history, the town of Alresford, Arlebury Park House and the surrounding estate are briefly introduced. Then, to provide a historical context, there is a short summary of some of the key events that shaped the world from the 1770s through to the 21st century. The different families who owned Arlebury experienced huge social, economic and political change: the importance of 'the landed gentry' in rural communities is described, together with some details about prominent members of the individual families who owned the estate, especially in its heyday.

In the 20th century, though, two world wars and the intervening Great Depression, meant that Arlebury was no longer tenable as a private residence owned by a single family, and the interior of the house was divided in 1945 into apartments. Nonetheless, the house, the converted stables and farm buildings (now The Mews and The Barns), the entrance lodges, the handsome boundary wall alongside the iconic Avenue (the old Toll Road, complete with Toll House), the formal garden, the walled kitchen garden area, the farm bailiff's house and the lovely parkland setting, with long views to and from the north Hampshire downs, remain in their *'perfect and compact ring fence'*[6]. Historic England calls this 'group value'.

Many fine country estates of both national and local historic interest have been demolished but some, including Arlebury, found new uses and so survive to this day.

---

[5] The limited-edition book 'A recent history of Hampshire', c. 1922, is a sort of 'Who's Who' of major properties in the county. J Looker Ltd., The Wessex Press, Poole.

[6] Facsimile of the 1846 auction documents. See Appendix 3 HRO Finding number 44M69/E22/1/2

Part 1: A brief introduction to New Alresford & Arlebury

Alresford was founded in 1189 – 1204 by Bishop Godfrey de Lucy and was an important medieval trading centre but re-building after several catastrophic fires resulted in a pleasing mix of mainly Georgian, Victorian and Edwardian architecture in the town centre today. The *original* Arlebury is Georgian (usually defined as 1714 to 1830) and was probably built between c. 1775 and 1785. It appears on Milne's 1791 map, marked with Wm. Harris's name (the founder of the estate) and on Greenwood's 1826 map, using its earlier name 'New Place'[7], as shown.

Figure 2 – Milne 1791

Figure 2a - Greenwood 1826

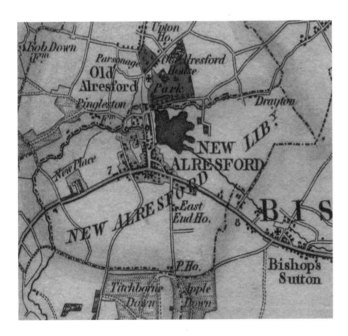

---

[7] Portsmouth University's collection of maps including the Milne 1791 and Greenwood 1826 maps can be found at http://www.geog.port.ac.uk/webmap/hantsmap/hantsmap

Victorian expansion of Arlebury

In Victorian times, largely after 1846, the house was greatly expanded, although the Georgian design was largely retained. The amount of agricultural land owned by the estate has varied hugely over the centuries but the historically important 'core' comprising the main house, stable yard, kitchen and formal gardens, the parkland and 'home farm' amount to about 105 acres.

Arlebury and the New Alresford Conservation zone

The estate was excluded from the main conservation area (i.e. the town centre and western approach, called The Avenue) when it was designated in 1969 (see conservation map below). This ensured a well-defined, reasonably tight conservation boundary, apparently the government instruction to Local Authorities at the time[8]. Standing about half a mile to the west of the town, parts of the house were in a poor state of repair when bought in the 1990s and restored by developers M25, and the adjoining Mews and farm buildings converted by Ashby Guion. The whole is now a well-presented part of the local heritage scene, surrounded by parkland and listed by the Hampshire Gardens Trust. The 2004 Winchester City Council Landscape Character Assessment notes that parkland is typically an historic feature in its own right, saying *'A large proportion of parks were created in the 18th century, when the construction of large country houses was associated with a designed landscape setting. Typical examples include Arlebury Park, Old Alresford House, etc.'*

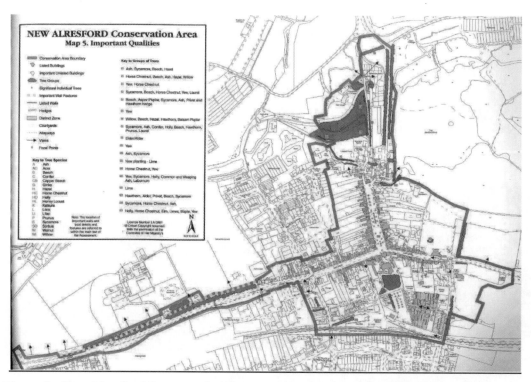

Figure 3 - New Alresford Conservation Area
Reproduced by kind permission of Winchester City Council

The Avenue

The Avenue, shown running slightly south-west from the town centre in Figure 3 above, was gifted to the town by the Bishop of Winchester, Charles Richard, in 1869. It was entrusted to the Bailiff and

---

[8] Alison Davidson, former Head of Conservation, Winchester City Council email to author 2014.

Burgesses and since 1890 has been in the care of the New Alresford Town Trust[9]. The Bishop attached strict terms: the land was to be used for the recreation of the inhabitants of the town '... *and for no other purpose whatever'*. There was a specific condition that no building or other erection of any kind was permitted and it is the responsibility of the Trustees to keep The Avenue as it was when gifted.

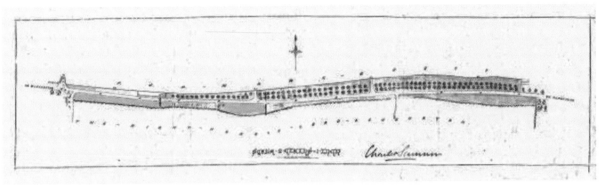

__Figure 4 - The map that accompanied the gift of The Avenue, signed by the Clerk, Charles Sumner__
Reproduced by kind permission of New Alresford Town Trust

The handsome flint and brick boundary wall (left of photograph below) is identified as an 'important wall feature' in the New Alresford conservation area. It probably dates from the early-to-mid 19th century[10] and forms the southern boundary of Arlebury Park, stretching from the edge of the town centre westward to Drove Lane. The wall and extensive planting of trees forms The Avenue and separates the estate from the 1753 toll road (to far left of photograph below). It ran from Southampton, to Winchester and Alton, and The Avenue remains the grand western entrance to the town. The town bailiff and burgesses had resolved in 1837 that *'The approach road from Winchester would be materially improved by the planting of elms or other trees on the wastes by The Turnpike Road'*. Landscaping took seven years and the trees (114, mainly limes) were planted in summer and autumn 1837-1844. The cost and care of the trees was the responsibility of the Bailiff and Burgesses and they did this for thirty years before the land itself was gifted by the diocese, possibly as a reward for a major project successfully carried out.

__Figure 5 - The Avenue; looking east towards the town centre__
September 2015

[9] Bailiff and Burgesses of New Alresford Borough. Hampshire Record Office: 7M74/DB1. The Town Trustees took over the assets and responsibilities of the Bailiff & Burgesses in 1890.
[10] Possibly 1835; a one-time resident of the East Lodge at Arlebury Park House has said that there is a plaque in the boundary wall showing this date but it has not, thus far, been found.

Part 2: Historical & social perspective

Over nearly 250 years, successive owners of Arlebury, their households, friends and neighbours were much affected by wider national and international events, sometimes directly, sometimes indirectly. When the land was bought for their new estate by William and Jenny Harris in 1774, the Industrial Revolution was accelerating, Captain James Cook was exploring the Pacific Ocean, and the American War of Independence started in 1775. The French Revolution (1789) spurred the Board of Ordnance into mapping the vulnerable south coast of England in detail so as to position military defences in the event of revolution spreading across the Channel. The battle of Trafalgar was in 1805 and in 1810 the first 1" Ordnance Survey map of Hampshire & the Isle of Wight was produced[11]. Waterloo was in 1815. During their lifetimes, the founders of Arlebury would also be directly affected by innovations in agricultural machinery and advancing 'enclosure' of land - to their great advantage.

Widespread upheaval throughout much of the 19th century was intended to change the political, social, and economic order. Less revolutionary than the experiences of many European countries, in Great Britain this period saw the 1832 Reform Act and repeal of the protectionist Corn Laws, and a radical move to free trade in 1846. This further altered the balance from an agricultural, landed society in favour of an increasingly industrialised one. William Harris died in 1817 but Jenny not until 1833, not long before Queen Victoria came to the throne (1837).

Before the Marx family acquired Arlebury in the mid-19th century, Arlebury was the property of two other wealthy owners, Richard Bailey (1812 – 1814) and then John Rawlinson (1814 – 1846) but little seems to have been recorded of their connection with the estate. The Marx family had 'feet in both camps': in both agriculture _and_ in City of London banking. During their occupancy, the Great Exhibition 'Works of Industry of All Nations' thrilled visitors to the Crystal Palace in 1851; the Crimean War started in 1853, the American Civil War in 1861, and Abraham Lincoln was assassinated in 1865. Thirty-odd years after the abolition of slavery in British territories, it was abolished in the United States in 1869 and, although flouted by various devices such as literacy tests and violent intimidation for many decades after, the 15th Amendment to the American Constitution gave the vote to black males in 1870.

In Africa, Stanley found Livingstone in 1871 with (reputedly) those famous words *'Dr. Livingstone, I presume?'* Supposedly, Livingstone responded *"Yes, and I feel thankful that I am here to welcome you.'* By the early 1880s, at much the same time as the Walford family bought Arlebury (1883), Africa and Indochina were colonised by competing European countries. Natural disasters included the catastrophic eruption of Krakatoa in 1881 in which some 35,000 people died. Jack the Ripper first struck in 1888. The first modern Olympic Games were held in Athens in 1896.

In 1901 the Victorian age closed and the stylish Edwardian era arrived with the new King Edward VII (1901-1910), a leading figure both here and on the continent. In 1901 the first wireless signal was transmitted by Marconi - from Cornwall to Newfoundland - heralding another turning point in communications. 1914 saw the start of the ghastly Great War. At the close of the war, universal male

---

[11] This was the first of the OS maps when still developed for ordnance purposes as opposed to later, more general use with the 1st edition dated 1867-70, depending on area covered. Maps for public use were expensive but immediately popular. For the first time (unless you were a hot-air balloonist), the country could be 'visualised' from the air and from 1855 early photography helped the map makers. 1870 saw the first 25" to the mile series and sheet 42.5 includes Alresford and Arlebury and details from it are reproduced later.

suffrage (at age 21) was introduced, alongside votes for *some* women (those over 30 who had certain minimal property rights). Younger women (21) had to wait until 1928.

The rural population & agricultural decline

The history of the Arlebury estate and its owners helps chart the huge changes from a largely rural society, through manufacturing, which came to prominence during the Industrial Revolution and then to the dominance of services, the law, public administration and finance[12]. At the turn of the 19th century, the urban/rural split had already changed dramatically from a hundred years earlier and the 2011 census for England shows 82.4% of the population lives in urban environments, 17.6% in rural areas. This is an almost complete turnaround in percentage terms since 1700.

Table 1 - % Urban/Rural Distribution

% Urban-Rural Distribution

Year	Urban	Rural Non-Agricultural	Rural Agricultural
1700	c.17%	c.28%	c.55%
1800	c. 28%	c.36%	c.36%
1900	c.77%	23% combined	

In 1801 (the year of the first census, albeit not a very precise one), the population of New Alresford was about 1132. In 1841, it was 1578[13] and in every census since then the percentage of people working in agriculture has declined.

Changing sources of wealth

There is a very considerable shift in sources of wealth over the lifetime of the estate. In William Harris's England, the main store of wealth (i.e. stock of assets) and source of income (rents, sale of produce, etc.) was agricultural land. Technical innovation and land 'enclosure' encouraged improvements in agricultural productivity to feed a growing population and it also released labour for industry: *'Only if a resource can be spared from the task of foodstuffs can a larger scale industrial production be attempted'[14].* The house and farm land owned by the estate were greatly enlarged in Victorian England under Francis Marx's direction, helping to bring in increased income from agriculture, alongside the family's substantial City banking interests. The Walfords (owners of Arlebury from 1883 to 1944) were descendants of an old established family and wealthy London solicitors, practising at 27 Bolton Street, Piccadilly. With the arrival of the railway in Alresford in 1865, access had become much easier and Arlebury was their country residence. But they were probably much less interested in and dependent on agriculture than their predecessors; indeed, the agricultural depressions in the 1880s and 1890s and again in the 1920s, sapped much income from farming.

20th century impacts on country estates

By the time of Henry Walford's death in 1928, World War I was over but the Great Depression loomed and World War II was not far distant. Added to the financial costs of war, the availability of servants had

---

[12] In 1841, 22% of people worked in agriculture & fishing and by 2011 this had fallen to <1%. Manufacturing was the most dominant in 1841 or 36% of the workforce, followed by services at 33%. The expansion of services and decline in manufacturing meant that in 2011, 9% worked in manufacturing, 81% in services. Key points from ONS '170 Years of Industrial Change across England & Wales', June 2013, 2011 census'.
[13] Social & Economic History Table of Population for New Alresford in A History of Hampshire Volume 6, p. 437.
[14] People, Cities & Wealth: the Transformation of Traditional Society, E A Wrigley, Basil Blackwell, 1987, p. 189.

been sharply curtailed, especially in terms of men, and women had been introduced to a widening range of exciting new prospects in commercial and public administration offices and factories; as drivers and technicians and in more senior teaching and nursing roles than ever before. They would never return to domestic service in previous numbers or on such low wages. As the upkeep of country house-living soared, many a family's private ownership of these properties became untenable. Now ruinously costly to maintain, many country houses had to find more viable uses. Arlebury Park House and estate were unsuccessfully offered for sale several times in the 1930s and 1940s and eventually sold in 1944. Perhaps the owners then, the Walfords, were also spurred on by Labour's threat of land nationalisation after WWII.

Some houses and estate buildings found new roles - converted to offices, as nursing homes, or were divided into flats and separate homes – as happened to Arlebury Park House and its outbuildings. Winchfield, near Basingstoke, built in 1760 and Grade II- listed, is now a wedding venue, another variation on the theme of new uses for old family mansions. Chawton House, Alton, an Elizabethan manor, is now a library and study centre for women's writing and was once owned by Jane Austen's brother, Edward Knight. Herriard House (*'a stately Queen Anne manor'*, dating from 1706), was largely demolished in 1966. Herriard was home to the Jervoise family for generations (closely connected to the Marx family by marriage) and they built a new house over the old cellars in 1970. Overall, nearly fifty country house properties were demolished in Hampshire alone. Some are retained in name such as Leigh Park in Havant (now, in part, the site of a housing estate[15]), others were destroyed by fire or by industrialisation, some were simply 'surplus to requirements' and knocked down[16].

Part 3: The 'Landed Gentry': public figures, employers, patrons, benefactors

Successive owners of Arlebury in the 18th & 19th centuries

The major owners of Arlebury in its heyday as a private family residence were, firstly, the founder, William Harris, who built and owned the estate (then called 'New Place') from 1774 to 1812, some 38 years. Richard Bailey owned it for just two years, 1812-1814. Then John Rawlinson owned it from 1814 to 1846, 32 years; the Marx family (who changed its name from New Place to Arlebury) from 1846 to 1883, 36 years, and the Walfords 1883 to 1944, some 61 years.

In 1808, William Harris had written to his nephew that *'he was not long for this world'* (see page 11) and in 1812 he sold the property, although it was not until 1817 that he died[17]. The new owner was Richard Bailey and dated October 1812, there is a rather incomprehensible attested copy (i.e. not the original but certified as a true copy) of *'the release and covenant to levy fine to bar dower of freehold or covenant to surrender copyhold estate called New Place estate'*. (See Appendix 6, for a further explanation of this).

---

[15] Part of Leigh Park, owned by Sir George Staunton prior to the housing estate being created, remained and is now the George Staunton Country Park, which may receive lottery funding to restore the landscape and associated follies, etc.

[16] http://www.lostheritage.org.uk/lh_complete_list.html

[17] The Harris family (parents and five children) were all buried in St John The Baptist's Church in Alresford, so their attachment to the town clearly remained.

Less than two years later, in April 1814, though, there are Articles of Agreement between Richard Bailey of New Place, Alresford and John Rawlinson of Combe, to sell '... *New Place and all its estate gardens, etc.'* for £14,000. New Place was a very substantial property and a detailed list of *'offices, garden and pleasure ground'* and parcels of land is given[18]. But the size of the total estate, including farm land, varied over the years and we don't know exactly what was included in 1812 (when Harris sold to Bailey), in 1814 (Bailey to Rawlinson) or 1846 (Rawlinson to Marx). Some further details about the Harris, Marx and Walford families are given in Part 4 but we know little of Richard Bailey, in particular, and not much more about John Rawlinson[19]. It is likely that neither lived at Arlebury permanently as both owned property elsewhere. There are advertisement for tenants of what was still called New Place, whether furnished or unfurnished, 'for the season or a term of years' in the Hampshire Chronicle and other local papers in 1818, 1819 and 1827; it was offered for sale or let in 1828 and 1832 before being successfully auctioned in 1846.

What was the 'Landed Gentry'?

None of the owners of Arlebury was a member of the aristocracy or a *'peer of the realm'* but they were all wealthy, part of the 'landed gentry' or rural 'ruling class', and their estates were the epicentre of their communities. They held public offices such as Deputy Lord Lieutenant of Hampshire, were magistrates, Justices of the Peace and burgesses. These people were considerably more important in the social hierarchy than larger tenant farmers (who rented their farms from the land owners) and much more so than a yeomen farmer, defined as *'a person qualified by possessing free land of forty shillings annual [feudal] value'.*

By comparison, senior public roles were qualified, as was the vote, by property; William Harris, for example, was qualified for his role as a Deputy Lord Lieutenant of Hampshire by right of £200 annual income and land. The landed gentry were 'pillars of the community' in many senses, not least because of their very great economic influence. They were significant employers of dozens of estate and farm workers, coachmen and grooms (later chauffeurs), gardeners, indoor servants and also seasonal and itinerant workers. They patronised the whole range of local professionals, businesses and tradesmen: from lawyers, doctors, bankers and clergymen to carters, wheelwrights, ironmongers, blacksmiths, fullers, local millers, saddlers, inn and shop keepers.

Members of the landed gentry were sometimes Members of Parliament, close friends with or related to them. Anna Maria Selina Locke Marx, wife of Francis Marx, was the daughter of wealthy banker Wadham Locke, MP for Devizes in Wiltshire, whilst several members of the Jervoise family (related by marriage several times over to the Marx family), were also MPs and Sheriffs throughout the 18th and 19th centuries. Through the second marriage of Constance Catherine Marx to Arthur Wood, the Marx family became linked to the rising class of prosperous industrialists. Sir Arthur was the son of John Wood, who used his wealth to invest substantially in property, as befitted a new member of the gentry. He had bought Shalden Manor in 1840 from Edward Knight (Jane Austen's brother) and also owned Thedden Grange, both near Alton, and was involved in the new Mid-Hampshire Railway line, opened in 1865.[20]

Until the arrival of the railway, travel over long distances was often difficult and uncomfortable, so links

---

[18] Hampshire Record Office: 11M65/1 & 2, 11M52/412, 413, 414, 415
[19] Like other owners of Arlebury, John Rawlinson too was a major land owner, Justice of the Peace and a Deputy Lord Lieutenant
[20] Hampshire Record Office: 4M51/443

between country house families tended to be within relatively easy reach, in villages and towns scattered in and around Alresford: in Old Alresford, Tichborne, Chawton, Thedden, Shalden, Winchfield and Herriard. The various families would have sought each other out as desirable and suitable alliances, as social, business and potential marriage partners[21].

There were also strong links with senior military officers and this area of Hampshire has been home to successive admirals, perhaps because relatively close to Portsmouth whilst also in the countryside. Admiral George Brydges Rodney (b.1719 – d.1792) used prize money to build Old Alresford House in the late 1740s and early 1750s. Two of Jane Austen's brothers, Admiral of the Fleet Sir Francis Austen (b.1774 – 1865), and Rear Admiral Charles Austen (b.1778 – d.1852), spent time at their brother Edward's estate at Chawton. Rear Admiral Frederick Wilbraham Egerton (1838 -1909) lived at Cheriton Cottage from 1885. Admiral John Locke Marx (b.1852 – d.1939, second son of Francis and Selina Locke Marx) was born and lived at Arlebury Park House throughout his childhood. Much more recently, Rear Admiral Morgan Morgan-Giles (b. 1914, d. 2013) was well-known in Alresford, as well as being an MP and Deputy Lord Lieutenant of the county.

It is in this context – the intertwined social, public and business lives of these families - that a brief note is provided as Appendix 2, regarding links between Jane Austen and the Harris family, as the families lived just 10 or 11 miles apart.

Part 4: A short history of the principal families at Arlebury up to the 20th century

As noted above, the Harris, Marx and Walford families were prominent local figures, significant employers and patrons, and benefactors of the poor and of the church (although *which* church later provides an interesting aside). John Rawlinson of Combe (near Andover) also owned the estate for many years but little is known of him in relation to Arlebury.

The Harris family - founders of Arlebury - 1774 - 1812

When William Harris married Jenny, nee Barnard, in 1770, they initially lived at 'Arclyd' in West Street in Alresford. In 1774, though, he purchased the Upper and Lower Stoke Closes, at the western end of Lower and Upper Brook Furlongs on the north side of the Winchester Road, leading down to the River Arle and marshes, from Robert ('Rob') Boyles (b.1723, d. 1782), Master of the Perins Free School in Alresford and a burgher of the town[22]. This is where Arlebury began, then called 'New Place', a mansion befitting an increasingly moneyed and noted public figure. Born in 1737, William Harris Esquire died a wealthy man in 1817, when it is recorded that he was *'possessed of about £24,000 personal property'*[23]. Depending on how you measure it, in today's money that could be c. £1.5m (in terms of the historic

---

[21] A History of the County of Hampshire, Vol.4, 1911, p. 101-103, and Elizabeth Martin, daughter of Sidney Martin, owner of Arlebury in the mid-20th century, has an old illustrated map (undated) showing several of these country houses, with links to the Hampshire Hunt, to which many members of the families belonged.

[22] Raymond Elliott, 'William Harris of Arle Bury'. Alresford parish magazine October 1986. Ms. copies and working papers Hampshire Record Office: 98A03/16. 'Arclyd' was 15/17 West Street, which became the Post Office.

[23] Prerogative Court of Canterbury. Until 1858 all wills had to be proved by church and other courts. The records show that *'William Harris, of New Alresford, in Hampshire, died in May, 1817, possessed of about 24,000l [£] personal property, leaving a will dated 13th of March, 1812, and a codicil of the 26th of October, 1815. Probate of both these instruments was granted in common form in July, 1817.'* See next page regarding the further codicil.

standard of living), £25m (in terms of economic status or 'prestige power') or even £80.5m (in terms of wealth relative to the total output of the economy)[24]. His will, lodged in the National Archives[25], shows that he left the bulk of his estate including an immediate payment of £5,000 from his personal estate and a further annuity, jewellery (diamonds, pearls and 'trinkets'), house, farms and lands ... to his *dear wife Jenny Harris'*. It might be assumed that jewellery, at least, was already the woman's property but even for much of the 19th century, property that women took into a marriage or acquired was legally their husband's. Once married, the only legal avenue through which women could claim or reclaim property was usually widowhood.

Remorseful after an earlier 'indiscretion', William had written a letter in 1808 to his nephew, Joseph Leacock, asking him to provide £1000 from his estate for his natural daughter, Louisa Denny[26]. William Harris wrote: *'My dear Joe, I find I am not long for this world; and shall, therefore, disclose to you a secret which is known to very few, though Mrs. Harris is acquainted with it. I have a natural daughter, by the name of Louisa Denny, who is now a teacher at a lady's boarding school, at Hampstead. I have bred up this girl with care and attention, and have given her a good education. I have not mentioned her in my will, because the world should not know of my indiscretion; but I desire you (to whom I have left all my property)[27] to pay within six months after my decease, to this young lady, one thousand pounds sterling, or allow her an annuity of fifty pounds per annum, from the day of my death. I further desire you will pay to her mother, whose name is Sarah Whitear, living in East street, in the town of Alresford ... an annuity of twenty-five pounds per annum, from the day of my decease, in quarterly payments. I have always found you to be a good lad; and I trust, as a man of honour, you will attend and follow the directions I have here given you, in the same manner as though contained in my will. P.S. I have a little money in the three per cent, consolidated funds which will enable you to discharge the above legacy and annuity.'*[28] When Wm. Harris died (although not until 1817), the nephew was in the West Indies and subsequently died himself, so the matter was referred to the Prerogative Court in 1818. The judge, Sir John Nicholl decided *'The codicil is in the form of a letter; but it is quite clear that the deceased intended it to be a confidential trust to his nephew not to be communicated till after his death. It was intended to operate independently of his will'. ... 'It was found uncancelled and unrevoked; and it has only been in consequence of the nephew's death that it has been necessary to bring it before the Court. I am clearly of opinion that it can operate; and that it was not intended to be revoked, notwithstanding the revocatory clause in the will, and, therefore, I admit [accept] the allegation'.*

Wealth & 'Enclosure'
Much of William Harris's wealth resulted from 'enclosure' of land (restricting its use to the owner so it was no longer available as 'common land'). This practice was centuries old but gained pace with the

---

[24] 'Measuring Worth' Advisory Panel, economists from UK & US Universities, established 2006
http://www.measuringworth.com
[25] http://discovery.nationalarchives.gov.uk/details/r/D236904
[26] In 'Reports of cases argued and determined in the Ecclesiastical Courts at Doctors' Commons Volume 2; and in the High Court of Delegates [1809-1821]'.
[27] It is unclear why Harris's will (written 1812 and proved 1817, after his death in May that year) shows he left his estate to his wife but the earlier letter (1808) states he left 'all his property' to his nephew. Did he simply change his mind four years after his initial letter to his nephew? Or, more likely, did he mean that his property would eventually come his nephew on Jenny Harris's death? That was not until 1833 but Joseph himself died in 1818.
[28] William Harris clearly thought highly of his nephew; there was some correspondence with 'Colonel Jervoise, Herriard House' the year before, in 1807, saying *'I have written to [Joseph] Leacock concerning your offer to [assist him] to a lieutenancy in the North Hants [regiment] and I have no doubt you will hear from him in a few days.'* Herriard Collection Hampshire Record Office 44M69/F10/41/4.

advance of agricultural practices and machinery that suited bigger fields. *'During the second half of the 18th century the landed classes were caught up by the idea of what was called at the time 'improvement'. They began to plan, drain and enclose, to run farms themselves and encourage their tenants to improve the farms that were on lease. This new interest, besides greatly advancing farming techniques, and boosting food output, enabled landlords to perhaps double their income. Once it became clear that this was the case, improvement became exceedingly popular'[29].*

It is recorded in the 1807 Alresford Enclosure Award (by Act of Parliament, a more legally watertight process and better recorded than more 'casual' enclosures), that William Harris farmed over half the arable lands in Alresford. In addition to the core of the estate – the house and immediate surrounds of c. 105 acres - this included land to the south, the west and north of the river in Old Alresford, in Medstead and Dorset. The total Award for Alresford covered 410 acres of open fields and marshland. Of 23 'allotees', William Harris and Sir Henry Tichborne received by far the larger shares (175 & 38 acres respectively)[30]. A copy of the plan of the parish of New Alresford (the parchment original is very fragile) and 'text of apportionment' says 'A rate for the purpose of defraying the expenses of the New Alresford Enclosures' meant that Wm. Harris paid the (huge) sum of £397 9s 1d and Sir Henry £58 10s 7d for their respective allocations. A 'further rate' (undefined but expenses again) says Harris paid £142 8s 3d and Sir Henry £20 19s 0d. Very large sums of money indeed at the beginning of the 19th century!

In addition to being a prosperous landowner (perhaps because of it), William Harris was made a _Deputy_ Lord Lieutenant of Hampshire in 1787[31]. The London Gazette also noted in 1789 that *'William Harris of New Alsford [sic]' was High Sherriff of Hampshire [then called County of Southampton]. He was a local benefactor to the poor and the church and a burgher of the town from 1773, serving for thirty years and as bailiff for seven years'*. The bailiff (akin to a mayor in a small town) was *'elected by the majority of the burgesses at an annual court, which they held for that purpose, in the month of August, when any vacancies that may have occurred among the burgesses are in like manner filled up.'*

The Harris family & the church
Committed Christians, William Harris and his wife Jenny[32] gave readily to the church and the poor. Set up in 1831 as 'Harris's Gift' and prior to her death in 1833, aged 85, Jenny left in her will *'an annuity in trust of ten pounds per year to be distributed forever to the poor on New Year's Day, in bread or other provisions, by the church warden or Overseers'.*[33] She left money for mourning clothes for her servants and further bequests of several hundred pounds to named servants. What was presumably the bulk of her estate is described thus *'... my personal estate I give and devise the same unto my niece Anna Maria Newbery absolutely forever and I appoint her sole executrix of this my will and testament in witness whereof I have set my hand and seal this first day of November 1831.*[34]*'* No indication of what the estate

---

[29] Mark Girouard, 'Life in the English Country House – A Social & Architectural History', Book Club Associates in association with Yale University Press, 1979, p.217.

[30] 'A Guide to Enclosure in Hampshire' provides a parish-by-parish guide. The volume traces the disappearance of open fields, common meadows, pastures and wastes, providing full details of all known parliamentary enclosures and formal written agreements. Where possible it also gives documentary evidence for informal enclosures and maps of many Hampshire parishes annotated to show former open fields and commons. 'A Guide to Enclosure in Hampshire 1700-1900', Hampshire Record Series, J Chapman & S Seeliger, 1997, p. 89.

[31] There were several _Deputy_ Lord Lieutenants at any one time; the sole Lord Lieutenant was usually titled.

[32] Jenny Harris: nee Barnard, youngest daughter of John and Mary Barnard, b. 1747, m. 1770, d. 1833.

[33] Jenny Harris's charity was amalgamated with several others for ease of administration into the United Charities of New Alresford, under a Charities Commission scheme, operating from 1923-1961. Closed 1996.

[34] Anna Maria Newbery (nee Woolls), daughter of Jenny's sister, married George Newbery of Yorkshire.

consisted has been found.

William Harris was granted two faculties by Winchester diocese; in 1783[35] for a family vault (the petition specifies the length, width and depth), and in 1797[36] for a gallery at the west end of St John's Church, as the family had no pew or sitting place, the church was thronged and they could only kneel to worship *'with much inconvenience'*. The vault was in the aisle of the church. When the church was re-constructed in 1898 (thanks largely to funds provided by a successor at Arlebury, HH Walford), the vault was left in place but the carved cover stone was reset in the organ vestry, where it can be seen to this day.

Deaths of the Harris children

By the late 18th and early 19th centuries, *average* life expectancy was about 40, skewed by the high number who died in childhood. Survive through your teenage years, though, and you had a reasonable chance of living into your 60s, 70s or 80s, as did both William and Jenny Harris.

Figure 6 - Memorial to Elizabeth Harris & her four brothers
©*Photograph September 2015*

All five Harris children died before their parents. To lose all five was probably unusual but mortality amongst young people – even in rural areas, far from Dickensian cities, and in wealthy families - was very high, only improving in the 19th century with better sanitation, clean water, better nourishment and medical care. The memorial, on the north wall of St John's, reads as follows:

To the Memory of

ELIZABETH HARRIS Daughter of William & Jenny Harris of NEW PLACE

Near .... TOWN

Who died the 20th April 1798

In the Seventeenth Year of her Age

Alfo to the Memory of Four Sons of the above named WILLIAM and JENNY HARRIS Viz.

WILLIAM who died the 25th of June 1773,

Aged 2 Years

WARD an infant

PHILIP died the 17th of February 1781, Aged 7 Years

And JOHN died the 28th of February 1789,

Aged 10 Years

---

[35] Hampshire Record Office: 261F/2
[36] Hampshire Record Office: 261F/3

The Eel House

It has been suggested that the wealthy Harris family built the Eel House, straddling the River Arle, in the 1820s. However, as noted earlier, Arlebury (then New Place) was sold by William Harris in 1812 (before his death in 1817) to Richard Bailey and, by the 1820s it was owned by John Rawlinson. William Harris's will says nothing on the subject but he left ample funds for his wife Jenny (who survived until 1833), so she could have paid for it. The black and white photograph below, taken from upstream (east) is thought to date from about 1870, although the man pictured is unknown. The colour photograph (from downstream, west) shows the largely restored Eel House in c. 2015. It had fallen into disuse but has been very substantially restored since 2006 through the continuing work of New Alresford Town Trust (which holds a 99-year lease on the property and opens it to the public several times a year), and The Alresford Society[37].)

Figures 7 & 8 - The Eel House

Photographs reproduced with kind permission of Alresford Heritage & New Alresford Town Trust

Alongside this stretch of river, a number of lakes and ponds were created. Several are of relatively recent construction but the oldest date back to the 18th century when they were *'created for the pleasure of the owners of Arlebury House'*. Perhaps these were the sorts of tamed 'wildernesses' that were popular then. They also provided local employment. It is said that Henry Herbert Walford provided work of a similar nature in the Great Depression. Jim Witchard was told by his father, who had bought the estate in 1944, that this work included *'bricking the side of the lake'*, presumably to make it more stable.

The Marx family – the growth of both house & estate, 1846 - 1883

Sale of Arlebury by William Harris to Richard Bailey in 1812 and re-sale to John Rawlinson in 1814 attract relatively little notice in the Hampshire Record Office but documents from 1846, when John Rawlinson died and the Marx family bought the property, are much more comprehensive. Commander Andrew Marx amassed quite a lot of material for a history of his antecedents, including family diaries. In 2013 Marx visited Alresford to talk to the Alresford Historical & Literary Society (Glenn Gilbertson, Chairman and Robert Fowler, Secretary) and to Jan Field (writer of this history and Chairman of The Alresford Society), and also met with Jim Witchard, who lived in flat number 6, directly under the Italianate Tower at Arlebury Park House. Sadly, Andrew Marx never got around to writing up a paper he promised to the

---

[37] This is now one of only a few remaining Eel Houses in the country. Its purpose was to trap mature eels at the start of their 3000-mile journey back to the Sargasso Sea. There they mate and die but the spawn is carried back on currents to rivers such as this to restart the cycle. Caught eels were sold in vast quantities in London.

Alresford 'Hist&Lit' before he died in January 2014. In several emails to me, though, he provided a few details, including a brief family history and family tree.

Dr MJ Marx (b. 1743, probably in Bremen, d. 1789), had six children who moved, after his death, to Richmond, Virginia with their mother. Only the eldest, George Marx (b. 1777 in Bremen, d. 1835) came to the UK. He was '... *possibly a city trader but appears as Senior partner in an American bank, Marx & Gowan [possibly Gowan & Marx Bank?], working with Baring Bros [evidence of close ties with the Baring estate in this part of Hampshire], selling US state and railway bonds'*.

Dr MJ Marx

I

5 siblings plus George Marx = 1st Selina Chambers = 2nd Mrs Johnson

I

6 siblings plus Francis Joseph Peter (FJP) Marx = Anna Maria Selina Jervoise (nee Locke)

I

George Francis Marx = Constance Catherine   John Locke Marx = Constance Lily Heath

George Marx married Selina Chambers and they had six or possibly seven children. When Selina died in 1826, George Marx re-married a widow, Martha Johnston, in a ceremony at Exton in 1828[38]. She was a member of the Smith family of Shalden, near Alton, just a dozen or so miles to the east of Alresford and whose previous husband was Arthur Johnston (m.1817 in Shalden)[39]. In her book on the naval life of George Marx's grandson, Admiral John Locke Marx, the author, Dr Mary Jones, identifies the second wife as 'Mrs Johnston of Shaldern' [*sic* Shalden] and says she brought 'the large country house property of Arle Bury at Alresford in Hampshire into the family'[40].

Biographer Andrew Marx mentions 'Mrs Johnson' [*sic* Johnston] in the brief family tree above. However, he believed it was George Marx's son, Francis Joseph Peter ('FJP'), not George's second wife who brought the house into the family, nearly 20 years later in 1846 when he purchased it from John Rawlinson. Andrew Marx's version is corroborated by a valuation of New Place done by Daniel Smith & Son of Pall Mall in 1847[41]. The valuation is to the effect that they had handled the sale of the New Place estate [later Arlebury] in 1846 to Mr Marx, and that they had advised the vendors acting for the late Mr Rawlinson, that the sale price of £7,300 was below the market value but that a quick sale was wanted and they understood Mr Marx had spent a very large sum on improving and repairing the property[42]. It seems slightly odd that such a valuation should be sought *after* the purchase but it is addressed to John Parkinson Esq., Grays Inn. As the previous owner of Arlebury, John Rawlinson, had died in 1846, it is possible that his estate was being settled and the enquiry was for the purposes of probate.

---

[38] Pallot's Marriage Index.

[39] Martha's brother, Thomas Smith was a witness at the marriage and the officiating minister was William Smith, most probably also a family member but little more has been found out about her in relation to the Marx family.

[40] A Naval Life: Edited Diaries & Papers of Admiral John Locke Marx 1852-1939. Ed. M Jones, Persona Press, Ch.1.

[41] Hampshire Record Office: 145M89/86; opinion of Daniel Smith & Son of Waterloo Place, Pall Mall.

[42] The handwriting of the valuation is barely legible in places but the figure of £7300 is clear, with a suggestion it was then in poor condition and that the executors of the estate of John Rawlinson (who owned New Place 1814 to 1846) wanted a quick sale. This might account for the price difference between 1846 and 1814, when Mr Rawlinson had first bought the estate for £14,000. However, it is not known what land, stock, equipment and machinery were included in the two sales in addition to the main property, so the figures may not be comparable.

FJP & Selina Marx

The oldest of George and Selina Marx's children was Francis Joseph Peter (b. 1816). 'FJP' married Anna Maria Selina Jervoise, daughter of MP Wadham Locke[43]. Hints in journals and letters, wrote Andrew Marx, suggest that she and Francis Marx were *'already quite well acquainted'* during her first marriage to George Purefoy Jervoise, MP and High Sheriff for Hampshire, and thirty years her senior, who died in 1847. Selina and Francis married in 1848. Their first son was George Francis and the second was Admiral John Locke Marx, of whom rather more later.

Anna Maria Selina Marx (known simply as 'Selina') had a rather famous younger sister, Frances (Fanny) Isabella Duberly (nee Locke, b. 1829), who visited Arle Bury often as the sisters were extremely close. In defiance of senior commanders such as Lord Lucan, who disapproved of wives accompanying their husbands to the Crimean battle fields (1853-56), Fanny, then 25, went there with her husband, Captain Henry Duberly of the 8th Hussars in 1854 and stayed there with him throughout. Described as '... a splendid rider, witty, ambitious, daring, lively, loquacious and gregarious', Fanny's vivacious presence amongst so many men caused a scandal; although the troops (who nicknamed her 'Mrs. Jubilee') admired her. Most wives at home criticized her; it was *'... no place for ladies'*.

Henry Duberly was relatively poor, as was Fanny herself, so she spent much time thinking up ways of making money, such as publishing her eye-witness account of the Crimean campaign. Fanny wrote home often, letters were leaked to the press causing much interest and so Fanny asked Selina to get her husband, Francis Marx, to edit the papers into a book. He did so, apparently toning down slightly the 'flighty' parts. Her lively 'Journal Kept During the Russian War', published in 1855 with a second edition in 1856, was quite a success.[44] Fanny had wanted to dedicate the book to Queen Victoria and it has been said she declined and snubbed poor Fanny at a regimental review.

Figure 9 – 'Fanny' Duberly astride her beloved horse 'Bob' in the Crimean war zone

Fanny often rode to the battle fronts, giving her a realistic understanding of the horrors of the campaign. Of Balaclava she said 'Even my closed eyelids were filled with the ruddy glare of blood.'

'Bob' was buried at South Warnborough Park, north of Alton, where friends looked after the horse following the return of Fanny and Henry to England. Back home with her sister, Fanny wrote *'I remember how beautiful I thought Arlebury was, the first morning I arrived from the Crimea and saw the thick, tender May foliage hanging over the mowing grass'*.

FJP Marx and the Volunteer Rifle Force

Francis Marx was a prominent local figure: made Justice of the Peace in the Michaelmas Session in 1849, the property qualification for this role is noted as *'... house and lands in New Alresford'*. In 1859 the

---

[43] The Hampshire Chronicle for 19th August 1848 noted: Married, on Tuesday, at Farnham ... Francis Marx, Arle Bury, to Anna Maria Selina, daughter of the late Wadham Locke ... and widow of the late George Purefoy Jervoise.
[44] Journal Kept During The Russian War: From The Departure Of The Army From England In April 1854, To The Fall Of Sebastopol. By Frances Isabella Locke Duberly (1829-1903). London: Longman, Brown, Green, and Longmans, 1856 (Second Edition).

Volunteer Rifle Force was formed to protect England from any possible invasion by Napoleon III. The safety of the south coast and Hampshire were, of course, central to this. A committee was formed, *'... including F Marx, Esq. of Arlebury'* and the 16th Hampshire Rifle Volunteer Corps was duly formed in 1860. The Lord Lieutenant of Hampshire, the Marquis of Winchester, *'... presented commissions to the leading gentry of the town with Francis Marx as 'Lieutenant in Command''*. A fortnight later, thirty-three men from Alresford and the district were sworn in. By 1861 there were over fifty men in the Alresford Corps. Francis Marx was highly regarded and later given the rank of Major, the first to be awarded in the Rifle Force[45].

'FJP' had many other interests too. He seems to have written articles on the Crimean War for The Spectator and, as noted above, edited his sister-in-law's letters from the battle fields into a successful book. During the famous trial concerning the 'Tichborne Claimant', Francis Marx was one of a group of local gentlemen who supported the view that the Claimant was genuine. In the sworn evidence of FJP Marx, JP for the county and Major of Volunteers, he concluded *'I have no doubt about his identity'[46]*.

Together with public duties and work on re- designing the estate - Andrew Marx says he was an architect and may well have been a 'gentleman farmer' in his own right as well as owning much farming land - he also hunted as a keen member of the famous Hampshire Hunt (the 'HH') and became its Secretary. He died in 1876 after a hunting accident that probably broke his spine (death certificate, Appendix 5).

Originally a Jewish family, the Marxes seemingly joined the established Anglican church at some stage (whether here or in the United States is unknown), and 'FJP' and Selina Marx are commemorated in the window in the Lady Chapel at St John's church in the town, shown in the photograph below.

Figure 10 – Memorial window in St John the Baptist's church, New Alresford
© Photograph September 2015

It is a little surprising, therefore, that eleven members of the family, including both Francis and Selina (who died before her husband in 1873) are recorded in a graveyard plan[47] of St Andrew's in nearby Tichborne. Appendix 7 gives details of the family memorial plaques in St Andrew's, including one for Constance Catherine, whose first husband was Captain George Francis Marx (see next page). She is said to have worn herself out nursing wounded WWI soldiers when she died in 1916.

Although St Andrew's is pre-reformation Anglican, unusually it still has a Roman Catholic chapel (dedicated for the Tichborne family). Was the Marx family Anglican but sympathetic towards the Roman Catholic faith? Or did the second generation of the family want to be buried near George

---

[45] Hampshire Record Office: TOP343/3/1, p. 55 – 58 of Regimental Gazettes; 'About Alresford', John Reid, 1988; T Stacey Cove 'History of the 1st Volunteer Battalion, Hampshire Regiments 1859 – 89; and R Westlake 'The Rifle Volunteers'.

[46] Pamphlet 'Opinions of Hampshire Gentlemen on the Tichborne Claimant'; Hampshire Record Office 72A04/C1/25

[47] St Andrew's graveyard plan lists Francis Marx and his wife, Anna Maria Selina; George, FJP's father, Selina, his mother and sister Henrietta; George Francis (FJP's son) and Constance Catherine, his wife, and others.

Marx, FJP's father, who died in 1835? Or was it simply a question of friendships with people of similar interests, especially the Hampshire Hunt, with its strong links to Alresford, Tichborne and Cheriton areas?[48]

George Francis Marx

Born in 1849[49], George Francis Marx was the elder son of 'FJP' and Selina Marx, and brother of Admiral John Marx. *'Captain George Francis Marx lived at Arlebury, Alresford, Hampshire, England. He gained the rank of Captain in the service of the 68th Regiment, Durham Light Infantry.'[50]* Andrew Marx said that he served in India and Malta, was a Burgess of Alresford and Bailiff for one year, sworn as a Justice of the Peace in 1877 (qualification *'freehold houses and lands in the parish of Alresford'*), and formed the Fire Service for the town in 1879. Having died young in 1883, 'probably of a fever caught abroad', Arlebury was sold to Herbert Henry Walford that year. It is interesting to note that George Marx had married Constance Catherine Jervoise[51] (b.1852, d. 1916) in 1877 and she presumably inherited the estate in 1883 but it seems that her brother-in-law, John Marx, sold it on her behalf. This was ten years before the Married Women's Property Acts were finalised and married women would only then gain full control over property in their own right[52].

Arthur Hardy Wood

After the death of George Francis Marx at just 34, Constance Catherine Jervoise Marx married Sir Arthur Hardy Wood in 1885[53][54]. He was born at Thedden Grange, Alton in 1844, son of industrialist John Wood. Arthur was a 1st Class Hampshire cricketer, captain in 1870 and 1883-5, and set up a respected Country House cricket team at Winchfield[55]. He was President of the County Club in 1886, a JP for Hampshire, Secretary of the Hampshire Hunt and, later, Master of Foxhounds, a strong connection with the fox-hunting Marx family. Part of the network of local county families, he was recorded in the 1881 census as living at Chawton House, Alton, previously owned by Edward (Austen) Knight.

Admiral John Locke Marx

The second son of Francis and Selina Marx, John (b.1852, d. 1939) *'spent a happy childhood at Arlebury with its spacious grounds and verandas'[56]*, until he joined the naval officer training ship, Britannia, in Dartmouth. He joined the 'Old Navy' as a cadet in 1866, when the British Empire was at its height and

---

[48] The HH inn (now a private house, is thought to derive its name from the Hampshire Hunt.

[49] The Hampshire Genealogical Society census record for 1851 in the Hampshire Record Office lists Francis Marx, aged 1, born New Alresford but there is no record of his parents, 'FJP' and Selina Marx at this address on the census date. It is possible the baby was left in the care of outdoor servants whilst the parents were away.

[50] Montgomery-Massingberd, Hugh. *Burke's Irish Family Records*. London, U.K.: Burkes Peerage Ltd, 1976.

[51] The Berkshire Chronicle recorded on 25th August 1877 'Aug. 16, St. Peter's, Eaton Square, by the Rev. Chas. Causton, rector of Lasham, Hants, George Francis Marx, of Arle Bury, Hants, late Capt. 68th Light Infantry, to Constance Catherine, daughter of F. J. E. Jervoise, Esq., of Herriard Park, Hants.

[52] The Married Women's Property Acts: prior to 1870 a woman was legally an extension of their husband and property was ceded to him on marriage. After 1870 married women could own property but not sell it and it was only in 1893 that married women had full control over property inherited or acquired through marriage.

[53] Halhed Genealogy and related family branches.

[54] The Hampshire Advertiser for Wednesday, 6th May 1885 read '... at All Saints, Alton: Arthur Hardy Wood of Froyle Park, Hants, to Constance Catharine, widow of the late Captain Marx of Arle Bury, Hants, and daughter of the late F. J. E. Jervoise of Herriard Park.

[55] Cricket Archives at http://cricketarchive.com/Archive/Players/6/6931/6931.html

[56] There is no record of verandas in either the 1846 or 1944 sale particulars but 'sun loggia' is mentioned, which could mean much the same thing. See also photograph Figure 32, page 39.

foreign policy was backed by 'gunboat diplomacy'. The 'New Navy', with its Atlantic fleet and highly structured officer corps was different. Having been retired in 1909 due to lack of fleet experience, John Marx re-joined when WWI broke out and was given a temporary commission in the RN Reserve in October 1914. He kept an extensive journal, edited by Dr. Mary Jones (who also had access to Andrew Marx's papers) in her book 'A Naval Life'.[57] In a review of her book, written by Dr. Andrew Lambert of King's College London, he writes how the war revived Locke Marx's career saying *'Commanding in decoy or 'Q' ships*[58] *he played his part in the anti-submarine war – delighting in the independence of his command, the challenge of finding the enemy and the camaraderie of the wartime Navy'*. Marx was awarded the CB (Companion Order of the Bath, the DSO (Distinguished Service Order) and MVO (Member of the Royal Victorian Order). A local historian recorded in the mid-1980s that *'Admiral Marx ... is well remembered in the Town'*[59]

The Walford family, 1883 - 1944

Herbert Henry Walford (b. 1835, d. 1928) bought Arle Bury in 1883 as his country residence and the family lived here for three generations until 1944. Mr Walford was the head of solicitors 'Walfords of Bolton Street' in Piccadilly and had a London town house at 6, Cornwall Gardens, Kensington, shown in the black & white photograph below. In the colour photograph (which is almost certainly the same mansion block, a tiny 218 sq.ft. studio flat (the combined living area – a bedroom, kitchen, plus bathroom) could have been yours when advertised in 2016 for £400,000.

Figure 11 - Walford's London house in Kensington & the same property in 2016

B&W photograph of the Walford London house reproduced by kind permission of Alresford Heritage

Herbert Henry Walford was elected to public office in 1894. The first Alresford Parish Council results (following the demise of the old system of Bailiff and Burgesses), say *'Mr HH Walford was successful with 87 votes'* and he became Chairman in 1896[60]. He was a Justice of the Peace for the County of Southampton, qualified *'by right of a freehold house and land in New and Old Alresford*[61]*'* and Second Senior County Magistrate for Hampshire.

Local historian, Raymond Elliott, wrote a number of papers in the 1980s about prominent citizens of the

---

[57] A Naval Life: Edited Diaries & Papers of Admiral John Locke Marx 1852-1939. M Jones, Persona Press, Ch.1.

[58] Heavily armed merchant ships with concealed weaponry, 'Q' ships lured U-boats into making surface attacks, when they were more vulnerable.

[59] Raymond Elliott for Alresford Parish Magazine, October 1986

[60] 'Shock Result at First Parish Council Election', Alresford Articles 2012, Brian Rothwell, p.5

[61] Hampshire Record Office: Q27/3/911

town, including William Harris[62] and Herbert Walford, who also provided the site on the south side of The Avenue where Perins School now stands and, from 1920 to 1938, the family lent *'the beautiful grounds of Arle Bury year after year for the purpose of the [Alresford] show ..'[63]*, advertised in the Hampshire Telegraph[64].

At Christmas 1928, '*Alresford lost a much-mourned local benefactor'* when Mr Walford died. The service at St. John's was followed by burial in the family vault in Kensal Green, London. He had donated a very large proportion of the money required to renovate the church in the 1890s, possibly five of the six thousand total, a sum that would now equate to c. £500,000. To undertake the work, he engaged the services of Sir Arthur Blomfield, the prominent Victorian church architect and Diocesan Architect for Winchester Cathedral. A petition was raised by the Parochial Parish Council for Mr Walford '*A benefactor of the parish'* and a faculty was granted for a bronze tablet to the right of the altar that reads '*In memory of Herbert Henry Walford to whom the restoration and rebuilding of this Church in 1898 was principally due.'* Then '*In 1902, due to the further generosity of Mr H H Walford of Arle Bury...'*, the stained-glass window depicting the Glorified Christ was installed, together with the reredos showing The Last Supper. The window was designed by the Powell family, owners of the famous Whitefriars Glass Works: nothing but the best[65].

Like the previous owners of Arlebury, Mr Walford was an important local employer; after WW1 he paid unemployed men to dig out ditches and parts of the lakes to the north of the estate[66]. He employed a butler[67] who headed an indoor staff of nine or ten, a chauffeur and groom, a head gardener, three under-gardeners and two garden boys. Like other wealthy families, though, the Walfords and many indoor staff moved back to Kensington for 'the season' from October until the spring, leaving only a caretaker behind. The gardeners, farm bailiff and seven farm workers stayed all year, working the grounds and fields, including land on both sides of the Winchester road, the water meadows and the river's fishing banks[68].

Mr Walford's friends and contacts were wide-ranging. Francis, 2nd Earl of Northbrook (of the Baring banking family, MP for Winchester) presented prizes at the Alresford Show. In September 1908 a major army exercise '*The Defence of England'*, involving '*nearly all the Army in the south of England'* was held in and around Alresford, with Lieutenant-General Sir Horace Smith-Dorrien headquartered at Arle Bury at the invitation of Mr Walford.[69][70] Brief reminiscences of the Rector of St Andrew's in Tichborne record that the church tower was the lookout for the senior commanders watching manoeuvres.

---

[62] 'William Harris of Arle Bury', Raymond Elliot, Alresford Parish Magazine, October 1986

[63] 'Herbert Henry Walford', Raymond Elliott, Alresford Parish Magazine, January 1987

[64] https://www.britishnewspaperarchive.co.uk/, search Arle Bury

[65] Information provided by local historian Peter Pooley

[66] Corroborated in discussion between the author and Mr Jim Witchard in November 2014

[67] Before the war, Charles Mercer, butler at Arlebury Park House lived, with his family, at the Toll House on The Avenue, then part of the estate (Lot 4 when sold in 1944 to Ernie Witchard).

[68] Op Cit. R Elliot 1986/87 and see file of research notes Hampshire Record Office: 98A03

[69] There is a much fuller account in 'Arlebury Park, the HQ for the Defence of England - British Army 'Utterly defeated' by Glenn Gilbertson, Alresford Historical & Literary Society 2011

[70] In 1908 the War Office was alarmed by possible European designs on the United Kingdom (as, indeed, governments and the military had been for centuries) and there was public alarm at '*a rampaging German army ... and provocative new [German] fleet'*. As at the time of the formation of the Volunteer Rifles under Francis Marx in 1860 (see page 17), strategically important sites were seen as potentially vulnerable, including the south coast of Hampshire.

Figure 12 - The granite cross, St John's, Alresford
© Photograph November 2015

Many of those who took part in such military exercises would be engaged in the real thing in the Great War. A WWI memorial had been intended to be erected at the top of Broad Street but Mr Walford used his influence to have it sited beside the church, where the granite cross stands today[71]. Mr Walford's grandson, Colonel Hugh Carr Walford, 17th/21st Lancers, would die in France in WW2 and is listed, with many other local men, on a memorial inside the church.

Aged about nine, Hugh Carr Walford is believed to be in the painting below, with his father Herbert Neville (H H Walford's son) & Hugh Selwyn Walford (H H's brother), on Arle Bury lake. The painting, dated about 1966, is by well-known country house and landscape painter Julian Barrow (1939 - 2013), after a photograph dated September 1910.

◀*Figure 13 - Walfords on Arle Bury lake*
The painting, done in the mid-1960s, was based on a similar photograph to the one below, dated about 1910. The actual photograph from which the painting was copied has seemingly been lost but this one was taken about the same time.

John Walford, writer of his family's history[72] told me in an email *'As for the painting by Julian Barrow of the two Walfords and their sons on the lake at Arle Bury, it is of course a bit of an anomaly. I commissioned the painting around 1966, as a bet with the artist, who at the time was a friend of mine. Julian Barrow, seeing the old photo of Sept 1910, bet me that he could make a painting of it within a couple of hours, and that I was to come round to his studio and, if he had in fact completed it, I was to give him a bottle of whiskey, as best I recall! And that's what unfolded.'*

◀ *Figure 14 - Walfords on Arle Bury lake*
Photograph c. 1910

Both painting and photograph reproduced by kind permission of John Walford.

---

[71] Personal communication from local historian and Church Warden, Peter Pooley, in 2015.
[72] Walford Family History at http://www.johnwalford.com/home/Walford_Family_History.html. When John Walford went to the USA he gave the painting to his brother, Michael Carr Walford of Wolverton, Hampshire.

Part 5: Post World War II & end of an era

The changing order: the 'Big House' up for sale again

We don't know the particular circumstances of the Walford family following the two world wars and intervening depression era but the upkeep of fine country houses often became prohibitive for purely private use around this time. The Walfords found the estate difficult to sell in the 1930s and early 1940s, when the property was offered variously as a private residence, as a sporting estate and then, in 1943, as 'Very suitable for Country Club or Hotel, School or other purpose, besides private occupation.'

Advertisements for Arlebury estate[73]

- **In 1933:** *'Highly recommended' by John D Wood & Co., Berkley Square, London – 'One mile exclusive dry fishing, with lake of four-and-a-half acres' and a promise of '200 to 250 lb. trout should be killed annually in river only'. 'Three-quarters of a mile from town and station [New Alresford station closed 1973]; 57 miles London. HAMPSHIRE Compact residential estate of about 150 acres. Excellent land together with this attractive residence. Two lodges. Seven cottages. Farmery. Practically all in hand. Electric light. Ample water. Central heating[74]. TO BE SOLD AT MODERATE PRICE'.*

- **In 1934:** *'Personally inspected and recommended by the agents, Curtis & Henson, Mount Street, London' - Eight miles from Winchester. London under 60 miles by road. Favourite sporting location. COMPACT RESIDENTIAL AND SPORTING ESTATE. The Residence is built in the Georgian style and is approached by two long carriage drives. Five reception rooms, billiard room, nine principal bedrooms, five bathrooms, excellent domestic offices and servants' quarters. Electric light. Central heating. Garage for four cars. Two lodges, home farm with seven cottages. Lake of four-and-a-half acres. About one mile of first class trout fishing in the river which intersects the Estate. The whole Property extends to over 150 acres. ADVANTAGEOUS TERMS.'*

- **In 1943:** *F. Ellen & Son, Andover, estate agent & surveyor's sale particulars for Arle Bury, Hampshire. 'Residence containing 17 bed rooms, 5 bathrooms, 5 reception rooms; electricity; 2 lodges 7 cottages; about a mile of excellent fishing, good shooting, farmery, 150 acres. Very suitable for Country Club or Hotel, School or other purpose, besides private occupation.'*

The successful 1944 sale to Mr Ernie Witchard

Eventually sold in 1944, the property stretched from Drove Lane in the west, along the length of The Avenue to The Dean abutting the town centre, consistent with the '105 acres' shown in sale records in 1846 (see 1943 survey map on the following page). The sale documents describe the 'Residential & Sporting Estate' as including 'RESIDENCE, TWO LODGES, SEVEN COTTAGES, FARMERY, LAKE, ABOUT A MILE OF TROUT FISHING, and CAPITAL SHOOTING'.

---

[73] Arle Bury, New Alresford: large house with sporting estate, 1933-43; HRO Finding Number 159M88/37
[74] Resident 1949 to 1977 at Arlebury, Elizabeth Martin doesn't recall central heating but it is mentioned in the 1944 sale (further details next page), so it is possible it was removed when the house was divided into flats in 1945.

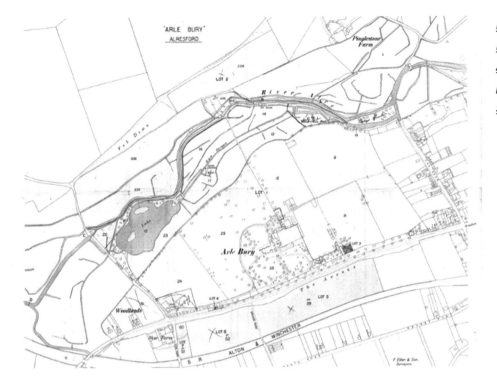

*Figure 15 - Survey by
F Ellen & Son of
Andover of Arle Bury
prior to its eventual
sale in 1944*

The 1944 sale lots

Lot 1 - The Residence

- o Dining room 26ft. x 23 ft.., smoking room 21ft. x 19ft. 6 in., library 21 ft. 6 in x 17ft. 6 in., billiard room 26ft. x 22ft. 6 in.[75], and services such as central heating and water 'pumped from the river by an automatic ram to the storage tanks in the tower on the east side of the House. The supply is abundant'.
- o Stabling [The Mews area] including nine loose boxes, harness room and, as horses were increasingly giving way to motor vehicles, a 'large garage 32ft. x 16ft.'
- o The farmery, including piggery, the bull house, cowshed and further stabling.
- o Pair of substantial brick and flint, tiled cottages [now Arle & Arlebury Park Cottages].
- o The East and West Lodges.

Lots 2-7

- o Lot 2 (nearly 9 acres) was at New England [across the river in Old Alresford parish] - two brick, flint and tiled farm cottages [now joined into a single dwelling called The Lodge], plus arable land.
- o Lot 3 was 'Trees'[76], 'the double fronted cottage, adjoining the main road [The Avenue}'.
- o Lot 4 was the Round House [in The Avenue; aka the Toll House, a Grade II listed building].
- o Lot 5 was 'freehold building land', half for immediate development, half temporarily restricted, lying opposite the east entrance to the house, between The Avenue and the railway line. Bounded on the west by Bridge Road, this is now the site of Perins school.
- o Lot 6 was also freehold building land 'about 6 acres' and 'scheduled eight houses to the acre,
- o temporarily restricted'.
- o Lot 7 'about an acre of garden, alongside the building land at New Road [New Farm Road].

---

[75] My neighbour, Sheila Mitchell, also recalls that the billiards room was in the basement, subsequently converted to provide two extra flats.

[76] Elizabeth Martin doesn't recall her father, Sidney, owning 'Trees', so it is possible it was sold off separately by Ernie Witchard in 1949 when he sold the rest of the estate to the Martins.

- There is also a schedule of the estate including the lake with boat house, park, water meadows, arable land and watercress bed.
- Outgoings are recorded, including 'present rates on House £93–14–6'.
- Vacant possession was to be given on completion bar a couple of tenants of cottages and 'the south sitting room, drawing room, library with the loggia and WC in the garden', requisitioned by the War Office for the Home Guard at a rental of £120 per annum.

The sale, coming just before the end of the Second World War, signalled that the halcyon days of many such properties were over. Ernie (or Edward) Witchard[77] had apparently only wanted the land for farming and a lady in the town (unnamed) had offered to buy just the house but this arrangement fell through. Besides farming, Ernest Witchard also ran a haulage business in The Dean and did his share of civic duty as well: '... *he was into all sorts of things*[78]. He was a magistrate in the 1940s and served on the Parish Council. Then in 1945, he started on a new use for Arlebury Park House, converting it into eight separate apartments, each running parallel, front to back, nos. 1-4 on the ground floor and nos. 5-8 on the first floor. Ernie's son, Jim, showed me a detailed set of working drawings and typed foolscap pages of accounts of monies for the building works paid to Musselwhite & Son Ltd. of Basingstoke, then with an office in The Dean[79]. The owner-manager then always wore a bowler hat and when asked by Jim as a boy why he didn't eat his lunch with his workmen he replied that *'I couldn't do that; sit and have lunch with them and then have to tell them off for something ...'*

Like his father before him, Jim Witchard had many roles: farmer, haulage contractor, fireman and New Alresford Town Trustee and, of course, family man and church man. He recalled that *'When his father bought the estate, the only residents were Mr Walford* [which one he couldn't recall but probably Herbert Neville, HH Walford's son]*, a cook and a chauffeur'*. Jim had been told lots of stories by older members of his family about the earlier heydays at Arlebury.[80] *'Back then, Arlebury would be thronged throughout the summer season with Walford family members, their servants, a succession of house guests and their servants. The nine principal bedrooms (total 17 including servant's bedrooms in the attics*[81]*), five bathrooms, and five reception rooms were in constant use, and the house was served with large kitchens and scullery, a game larder (especially for wildfowl), plus a wash house for laundry and a dairy. The water tanks in the tower, supplied from the river, provided water to the property and the house generated its own electricity. In addition to 'live in' or 'in door' staff, others included about 5 gardeners, grooms and coachmen (chauffeurs later), plus workers who looked after the dairy, hens, pigs, sheep, cows and farm horses, and other farm labourers. They were accommodated around the stables, the piggery and the ram shed, or in the farm cottages or 'lived out'. The stables housed the riding and carriage horses (the heavy work horses were kept separately), and they and the carriages were washed down under the large archway that still separates the house from the mews courtyard.'*

Sold again - the 1949 sale to Mr Sidney Martin
Jim Witchard described his father, Ernie, as having 'itchy feet' and the family moved many times when

---

[77] Both names 'Ernest Edward' and 'Edward Ernest' are given because the information on the birth and death certificates were, according to his son, Jim, not quite what the family had expected to see. The registered name was Edward Ernest but he was always called 'Ernie'.

[78] Conversation Elizabeth Martin and author, January 2016.

[79] A request will be made to the family to secure these and other papers for the Hampshire Record Office.

[80] Conversations Mr Jim Witchard and author 2014 & 2015

[81] The family servants' names were scratched on slates in the attic

Jim was growing up, albeit within the local area. There was seemingly no particular reason for it but in 1949 the family moved to Jacklyns Lane, and Arlebury House and the surrounding land were sold to Mr Sidney Martin, possibly for about £6,000. The farm stock was also sold at auction by James Harris & Son of Winchester, announced in a *'Catalogue of Important Sale of FARMING STOCK including The Attested Herd of 50 Guernsey Cattle'*. The cows were all listed by names ... *'Tessie, Dimple, Myrtle, Buttercup ...'*. A hand-written note on the catalogue gives prices paid: *'for implements (including three tractors and two lorries) £1912 - 15 - 6; cart horse 'Sally' £48 - 6 - 0; cattle (Guernseys and others, including two bulls) £2563 - 1 - 0; pigs £367 - 0 - 0; poultry £68 - 2 - 0, totalling £4959 - 4- 6.'*

The Witchard and Martin families were close. Elizabeth Martin believes that her father, Sidney, and Ernie Witchard may have met at an evangelical 'tent meeting' in Alton, where the Martins lived then. Sidney may have been a member of the 'Open Brethren', allied to the Plymouth Brethren but, unlike the 'Closed Brethren', part of a network of 'assemblies' that met with other, like-minded groups. Ernie Witchard, like son Jim, was a staunch Methodist, so their nonconformist beliefs would have been an important link with the Martin family.

Sidney Martin began farming in Alton with four cows and a few acres of pasture, selling milk door-to-door. He prospered and, when he bought Arlebury, he moved in on Friday, 13th October. As a strict church man, Mr Martin had no truck with superstitious nonsense! Work on a Sunday, though, other than feeding and watering the animals, was not allowed. The Martins - Sidney, wife Annie Gwendolin[82], sons Peter, Russell and George, and daughters Elizabeth and Mary, lived in Flat 6 under the tower and what is now called 'Butlers' adjoining it, which faces into the stable yard. Elizabeth Martin remembers this well; her father kept hackney ponies, and winning trophies and rosettes were kept in glass cases in the stables. Whilst talking about the importance of horses then, Elizabeth was also reminded of re-enactments of the 'four-in-hand' stagecoach run from London to Southampton. This event happened several times, probably in the mid-1950s, and the horses were rested in the Arlebury stables.

The 1934 sale particulars (unsuccessful) and 1944 details (successful) both mention the billiard room in the large basement and the table was still there in 1949 when the Martins moved in. The boys were allowed to play on the table occasionally with other local lads, bringing in a few bottles of 'Tizer' but no alcohol was allowed. The table was eventually gifted to a boys' club in Alton. Under the billiard table was an auxiliary pump for the water supply; a ram pump pushed water uphill from the river and the auxiliary then pushed water to the tanks in the tower. Occasionally the system failed - a trout would be the cause, blocking the flow!

Sidney Martin didn't alter the main structure of the house but installed the modern farm buildings, including a new milking parlour. Once he gave up keeping hackney ponies, his daughter Elizabeth recalls that most of the original stables became garages at the bottom of the mews yard for tenants in the house, plus another two or three garages by the archway. (Cars were very much smaller and were actually kept in garages then!) The stable in the centre was a useful implement store. There was a flat above, probably used for the groom and Elizabeth remembers a Mr & Mrs Thatcher there when she was a child; he worked on the farm and she in the house and garden from 9.00am to mid-day.

Elizabeth Martin also recalls that the kitchen garden (centre of photograph below and left of the line of

---

[82] Annie and Sidney were 'always a great team' (says daughter Elizabeth) and Annie's maiden name was Harris. But the family came from Devon and there is no known connection with William Harris and family.

stables) included a 'pineapple pit', a method invented by Victorian gardeners for growing pineapples in colder climates. It consisted of three trenches covered with glass, slightly below ground level, connected with two cavity walls. The outer troughs were kept filled with 15 tons of fresh horse manure, which gave off heat as it decomposed and the pineapples were grown in the central trough, at an artificially high temperature. This required a lot of manual labour, which became more expensive, and as use of horses for transport declined, so too did supplies of manure and, therefore, pineapple growing. The introduction of steam ships in the later 19th century also meant that such fruit could be readily imported from overseas. The adjacent buildings also included a boiler house for the greenhouse and potting shed.

Sold again – back to the Witchard family!

Following the death of his wife Annie in 1970, Sidney Martin apparently felt he couldn't settle in the main house again, so sold it and about 8 acres of the land back to the Witchards in 1976-7 and moved to West Lodge, where his daughter Elizabeth still lives.

AERIAL VIEW OF THE ESTATE

Figure 16 - Photograph dated about 1976 *Original source unknown but probably part of sale particulars when sold by Sidney Martin back to Witchard family*

The 1990s and the developers arrive!

Developers saw attractive business opportunities at Arlebury in the 1990s.

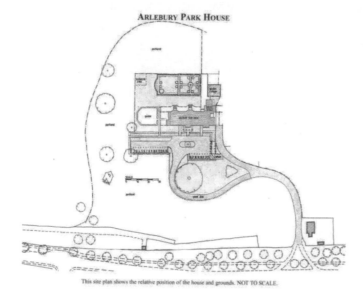

This site plan shows the relative position of the house and grounds. NOT TO SCALE.

Figure 17 - Detail from M25 sales brochure 1995

Ashby Guion Ltd. first converted The Barns, about 1992/3 and the stables and coach house (now The Mews) in 1996. The outline sketch here shows the main house, acquired by developers M25 Ltd in 1995 when they revised and upgraded the existing eight apartments and added four more, including converting the basement. (See Appendix 8 for a very brief note on the interior of the main house.)

The sketch above is undated, reproduced from the sales brochure but note that part of the old drive from the west lodge is still shown. Elizabeth Martin says that this entrance was used by some visitors in her father's time (1949 to 1976/7), rather than the east entrance. It was also *'the tradesmen's entrance'*, with an arm curling round to the back of the house for deliveries. Although now grassed over, Elizabeth thinks there is still a length of unmade track just inside the wall that leads to West Lodge.

The old turning circle for carriages in front of the house (Figure 31) is now a humdrum car parking area, whilst land west of the house was excavated to site garages. It was a planning requirement that they should not spoil the setting of the property, so initially had grass roofing to blend better into the landscape but this caused constant leaks and was eventually replaced.

The 21st century - saving Arlebury Park House again!

Arlebury Park House was saved from the possibility of neglect and even demolition in the 1940s when converted to flats. Some seventy years later, on February 12th 2015, two small fields front and back of the house were purchased by a consortium of the residents of the house and mews cottages[83] to prevent housing development. Following conversion work on the main house in the 1990s, developers M25 had retained the fields for future use and the front field was offered to Winchester's Strategic Housing Land Availability Assessment, part of the Local Plan 2011-2031. It is Winchester District policy to retain historic landscapes, saying *'... restoring registered parklands for the importance of their design or their place in the local landscape [is important]. To build would remove this objective.'*[84] Arlebury is a Hampshire-listed park, so it is unlikely that planning permission would have been granted but policies change and residents wanted to preserve the setting of this important part of the local scene. In 2018, though, there was another call by Winchester for available sites for housing development to 2036 and again, the front field was offered for development – unbeknownst to us, the owners. The developers acknowledged they did not own the site but claimed that they had the owners' consent! This was, of course, successfully challenged but we stay vigilant.

Part 6: Changing design & layout of Arlebury over the centuries

In the 2010 revised edition of *'The Buildings of England: Hampshire: Winchester & the north'*, the famous architectural series founded by Nikolaus Pevsner, there is this entry on Arlebury Park: *'Stuccoed Italianate house with a three-storey tower, begun in the mid-19th century. Its long elevation has two pediments[85], that to the right must have been central originally, the left part added some time after 1870. Large columned porch in the centre. The site was first occupied by a house of 1774 for William Harris. Its park was extended the full length of the Avenue in the late 19th century.'*

Based on evidence from the Hampshire Record Office (drawings and sale particulars, 19th and early 20th

---

[83] Arlebury Parkland Ltd.
[84] Winchester City Council Landscape Character Assessment, 2004.
[85] A pediment is a classical architectural design feature; a triangular section above the horizontal structure, often supported by columns. Georgian architects and builders often used this design as part of the main front door on housing or on the gable end of large buildings.

century Ordnance Survey maps), parts of this description seem doubtful and might better read: *'Stuccoed house with an Italianate three-storey tower. Viewed from the south-facing front, its long elevation has two pediments, that to the <u>left</u> seems to have been the original house built for William Harris after he acquired the land in 1774, and the <u>right</u>-hand part added later in the Victorian era, the tower possibly after 1870. Large columned porch in the centre. Its Hampshire-registered park extends the full length of The Avenue.'*[86]

We can now explore in more detail how the original, much more modest house gradually became the much-extended property here today. Whilst Arlebury remained in the hands of single, wealthy families - and manual labour, craftsmen and servants were plentiful and cheap, grand building and landscaping projects were popular. Some were of practical value, some carried out for pleasure, to be 'in the fashion', to display wealth and - just like today - to add value to the property. The house was extended greatly to the east, probably from 1846, whilst the stables were enlarged to keep pace with the growing establishment and many visitors. Presence was later added by the Italianate Tower, the entrances were re-designed to show the property off to greater advantage and gate houses built.

In the beginning ... what New Place was like

Arlebury Park House was originally called 'New Place' when building commenced in the mid-to-late 1770s and/or early 1780s. There are no indications that William Harris further developed his house before he sold in 1812 to Richard Bailey. It was soon re-sold to John Rawlinson in 1814 and there is newspaper archive evidence of attempts to sell or let the property in 1819 and in the late 1820s but nothing has emerged suggesting any major re- development of the house itself before it was finally sold again in 1846 to the Marx family[87]. Francis Marx, seemingly himself an architect, started to introduce significant change that would greatly expand the property, both the house and stables, and, according to his biographer, Commander Andrew Marx, using family diaries, acquired much additional farmland as well.

The 1846 sale particulars below refer to 'New Place' but the Ordnance Survey map dated 1870 specifies 'Arlebury House', so the name clearly changed sometime after the Marx family acquired it.[88] The first known visual impression of the house appears to be the mid-19th century sketch shown below, prepared for sale of the property by Daniel Smith & Son, Land Agents, in 1846[89]. The sketch is of a pleasing, well-proportioned but *relatively* modest country house, with just the single pediment. The style is fairly typical of Georgian domestic architecture: square, symmetrical, three storey, with what appear to be six panel windows, which would have been sash operated, with internal shutters.

---

[86] Pevsner also goes on to say *'Nearby, The Round House, a former toll house of c. 1753'.* However, whilst the toll road itself dates from 1753, the current toll house is Victorian.

[87] Although the house itself may have been unchanged by previous owners, the auction papers 1846 (Appendix 3, pages 50 & 51) speak of 'well-planted grounds' and 'ornamental plantations', so the 'pleasure garden' and parkland obviously pre-dated the sale to the Marx family and could have been the work of John Rawlinson, who owned the property from 1814 to 1846. There will, though, always have been a kitchen garden from the earliest days of the house, providing fruit and vegetables. (See Part 7 for further details on the garden).

[88] The name 'Arle' (or Alre) presumably relates to the name of the town and river but 'bury' is a corruption of 'burh', 'burough', etc., meaning 'fortified place' or just 'wall', so there may be some archaeological link. Perhaps the name was chosen simply because the owners liked the sound of it.

[89] A copy of the entire sketch, which includes the surrounding park, is given on page 36 and original parts of the sale particulars are in Appendix 3. Jervoise of Herriard Collection: Hampshire Record Office: 44M69/E22/1/2

Figure 18 below – Detail from original sketch prepared for 1846 sale

Figure 19 below – Photograph of same portion of the house today

The 1846 auction details

PARTICULARS

OF THE ABOVE VALUABLE FREEHOLD PROPERTY, COMPRISING THE MANSION OF NEW PLACE
THE PROMINENT FEATURE AMIDST THE PICTURESQUE SCENERY ON APPROACHING
THE TOWN OF ALRESFORD FROM WINCHESTER

From Messrs. Daniel Smith & Son, Pall Mall, the advertisement for sale by auction at The Mart,
near the Bank of England 'Unless an acceptable Offer shall be previously made by Private Contract'.

'New Place Estate and 105 acres of land with a trout fishery near Alresford .....The mansion of New Place to be sold at auction 18th September 1846 surrounded by well planted grounds, having an important frontage upon the highroad, from which it is screened by ornamental plantations; together with an estate in a most perfect and compact ring fence of about 105 acres, part very valuable water meadows ... [allocated to William Harris in the Enclosure Act 1807] ... extending to and embracing the river, which bounds it on the lower or north side for about a mile, affording some of the best trout fishing in the county.... Possession may be had of the mansion, gardens, paddock, fishery, etc., at Michelmas next, when Lady Paxton's lease expires'[90].

Changes and embellishments

Comparing the 1846 sketch (Figure 18, previous page) with later photographs (see cover and Figure 20, for example), demonstrates how the original house was expanded once acquired by Francis Marx. Using family diaries, FJP Marx's biographer, Andrew Marx, described the original property as a 'modest house' and added the query 'neglected?' He also says that Francis Marx, apparently an architect, *'...set about constructing a country estate ... They appear to have enlarged it by 200%, bought quite a large piece of land (from the Barings?) possibly as large as 400 acres, added the tower and much else'.*

The 1870 25" OS map covering New Alresford (sheet 42.5) shows how the Marx family introduced significant change to Arlebury, both to the house itself and the grounds. The original, straight driveway shown in the 1846 sale sketch (Figure 26) was replaced by successive, much more curving entrances over the years. A separate drive off the Avenue, east of the main entrance, was created to give access to the 'farmery' that was located to the north-east corner of the main house, beyond the stable yard and kitchen gardens. (The *original* working farm – noisome, muddy - had been about a quarter of a mile to the east on the edge of the town, just off The Dean).

In addition to the new driveways and the farmstead, the Marx family greatly enlarged the house itself. The long Victorian extension - albeit still in the Georgian style - repeated the original pediment, and the Italianate Tower was added. No specific date has been found for the latter but it is possible that Pevsner's comment *'added some time after 1870'*[91] is based on the 1870 OS map, which does not suggest the building had developed to its full extent at that time and, therefore, would not include the tower, which is at the extreme eastern end. FJP Marx died in 1876 but if he did not add the tower himself (as biographer Andrew Marx suggested), he may have left plans for further work, completed after his death. It is not until we get to the mid-1890s that the full extent of the house is shown on the OS map, so it is also possible that the Walford family was responsible for part, at least, of the expansion after 1883 when they acquired Arlebury.

---

[90] Lady Paxton was the daughter of Sir Wm. Paxton of Middleton Hall. She leased 11 acres including the house and pleasure grounds shown in the 1843 tithe award. She was also associated with Hoddington House, a Grade II* listed House in Upton Grey, Hampshire. The papers of George Purefoy Jervoise of Herriard (first husband of Anna Maria Selina Marx), includes a letter written to him by Lady Paxton in 1829, providing further evidence of connections between local families.

[91] 'The Buildings of England: Hampshire: Winchester & the north'. Michael Bullen, John Crook, Rodney Hubbuck, & Nikolaus Pevsner. Revised 2010, for the Pevsner Books Trust by Yale University Press

Figure 20 – Front view from the south- west - *Photograph September 2016*

The photograph above displays the 'finished' property well; its external appearance is largely unchanged since the early 1900s, as can be seen in the black & white photographs on pages 38 and 39. Working from left to right of the photograph above, we can see the original pediment (identifiably the same house as shown in the 1846 sketch, page 29) and the original entrance up the small flight of steps. This is followed by the large front porch, then the second pediment, and the later addition of the Italianate Tower at the eastern end[92].

The Italianate Tower

Although he was mainly writing about much more aristocratic establishments than Arlebury, architectural historian Mark Girouard, author of *'Life in the English Country House'* said that *'to make a house lop-sided [non-symmetrical] was a positively meritorious gesture, an escape from artificiality.'* Such fashions spread to less elevated levels of society but ones which could, nonetheless, afford such flourishes. The Italianate Tower, a 'belvedere' (or 'fair view'), overlooking the whole valley of the Arle to the north and up to the rising Hampshire chalk down lands beyond, combined a 19th century love of 'looking out on nature' and an architecturally striking addition; a way of saying 'We are in the fashion …'. As noted above, this example was probably added after 1870 as the OS map does not show the final, eastern extension of the house (and, therefore, the tower) but by 1896, the building is complete.

---

[92] The steps in the photograph (Figure 20) bridge the dry moat that lets daylight into the basement flats added in the 1990s.

Figure 21 - The Italianate Tower[93]
Photograph September 2015

The very distinctive tower was designed to add ornamentation (and demonstrate wealth) but another, primary purpose was to house a tank for water pumped from the river by hydraulic ram, so that water could then be piped through the property. Popular in country houses and estates in the 19th century, such technical innovations improved comfort and convenience for the family and guests, and increased the efficiency of running a large establishment. The tower at Arlebury was possibly modelled on similar ones (much grander, of course) at Queen Victoria's summer home, Osborne House, on the Isle of Wight.

Figure 22 - Osborne House, Isle of Wight, by master builder Thomas Cubitt

No direct evidence has been found that the famous master builder of Osborne House, Thomas Cubitt[94], was in any way involved in the design and/or building of the tower at Arlebury but there are two interesting connections. Firstly, Francis Marx started upgrading Arlebury shortly after he bought the estate in 1846, around the same time as Osborne House was being built (1845-1851). The Marx family had apparently bought the first lease on 81 Eaton Square in London from Thomas Cubitt, who had

---

[93] The Italianate style was developed in Britain at the beginning of the 19th century by John Nash and popularised by Charles Barry (Houses of Parliament) in the 1830s. Sir Charles was a great promoter of the style, admiring *'...the charming character of the irregular villas of Italy.'*

[94] Cubitt was much esteemed by Queen Victoria who, after his death in 1855 said 'In his sphere of life, with the immense business he had in hand, he is a real national loss'.

started designing the area about 1826 for the famous Grosvenor Estate[95]. Letters to Miss Mary Marx from the Jervoise family of Herriard House in 1839, show this as her London address. Not *quite* as socially desirable as Mayfair and Belgrave Square, Eaton Square was, nonetheless, an extremely well-to-do location[96], underscoring the significant affluence of the Marxes, a banking family as well as being landowners. (Just around the corner, incidentally, in Eaton Place, is the (real) town house inhabited by the (fictional) Bellamy family in the TV series *'Upstairs Downstairs'*. Like Arlebury Park House, the *'Bellamy House'* too has been divided into separate flats.)

Secondly, Charles Kingsley (1819 - 1875)[97], chaplain to Queen Victoria, is also said to have stayed at Arlebury frequently, possibly when he was Rector of Eversley, Hampshire, from 1842[98]. Appointed as Chaplain at Osborne House in 1859, it is possible that he took the idea of the Italianate Tower to Arlebury when he visited. A letter from Charles Kingsley to Francis Marx in April 1869 made arrangements to meet in Winchester but it provides no further information that helps to date the expansion of the house and particularly the tower, which Pevsner thought should be dated after 1870[99].

Horsepower & The Mews

Horse power was virtually the sole means of transport in the 18th century countryside and for much of the 19th until the railway arrived in Alresford in 1865.

Figure 23 - In memory of 'Comet' and 'Hilda' Photograph November 2016

Horses such as 'Comet' and 'Hilda' were great favourites with the Marx family, commemorated in this photograph of a stone plaque on the inside of the boundary wall fronting Arlebury Park House.

Elizabeth Martin, whose family owned Arlebury 1949 - 1977, also told me about a horse that supposedly took part in the famed 'Charge of the Light Brigade' and was buried or, at least, commemorated by a large stone somewhere at Arlebury. FJP Marx was owner of the estate during the Crimean War. It is noted earlier that he edited his sister-in-law's account of the war, and notes by his biographer, Andrew Marx, suggest he may have written in The Spectator about the conflict and was,

---

[95] Emails and conversation author with Andrew Marx (FJP Marx's biographer) in 2013.

[96] The Marx family had the lease on 81 Eaton Square where a 2 bed-roomed flat now costs about £2,800,000. The National Archives show that the Duke of Bedford was at this address in 1876.

[97] Kingsley was also a university professor, social reformer, historian, author ('The Water Babies' and 'Westward Ho!') and a friend of Charles Darwin and early supporter of theories of evolution – unusual in a clergyman at the time.

[98] Victoria History of the County of Hampshire, Vol.3, p.350.

[99] Jervoise of Herriard Collection: Hampshire Record Office: 44M69/F19/4/7.

perhaps, a member of the 'Turkish Association'[100]. So, the story about the Crimean warhorse is not, perhaps, totally improbable; could one or both of these horses have been in the Crimea … the dates tally?

Horses were also very important as producers of natural fertilizer! The stables have always adjoined the main house, slightly to the north east[101]. The adjacent kitchen gardens (with much of the high, red-brick garden wall still intact today), were just behind the yard and recipients, no doubt, of loads of horse manure for growing the fruit and vegetables. In the 1870 OS map it looks as if the yard has been further developed and by 1896 there are more stables to the east.

The farm, estate offices & The Barns

Accompanying the 1846 sketch and sale details for the *'mansion, pleasure grounds and garden'* (Plot 69), is a note of the other main areas around the house. Plot 68 (to the east of the entrance) is *'The garden paddock'*, Plot 70 is *'The lawn'*, stretching beyond the garden down towards the river and other surrounding plots are arable, pasture or river. Plot 64 was called *'Dean Paddock'*, described as pasture but the entry also goes on to say *'In No.64 is a spacious farm yard, two large barns, cattle sheds, etc.; and there is a brick and tiled fishing house in the meadows'*. The latter is the Eel House (see page 14) and 'Dean Paddock' is clearly the working farm mentioned previously, before it was relocated closer to the main house, possibly in 1862 when the original site was used for the new town gas works. 'FJP' Marx probably got a good price for selling or leasing the land for this purpose.

The relocated farm, much closer to the main house, may have been a 'model farm'; a 'gentleman farmer' (a wealthy person not reliant on income from farming), would be able to speak of 'my farm' and follow an interest in the latest in scientific methods in agriculture that helped boost productivity to feed the country's growing population. The courtyard layout of the new farm at Arlebury (see 1870 map, page 36) was quite typical[102].

The Barns

The 1870 OS map shows a new driveway[103] leading to the new 'model farm'. This was later the site of Sidney Martin's farm in the middle of the 20th century and the buildings around the courtyard were eventually converted in the 1990s to become what we now call 'The Barns'. At the end of the driveway (seen in the distance in the photograph below), the drive bends sharply left, past semi-detached Arle

---

[100] With France and the UK, the Ottoman Empire fought the Russians in the Crimean War (1854-56)

[101] A brick pier in the wall west of the stable yard bears a date of 1851, implying that this was when some work was completed on this area. This date fits well with expansion of the house and estate by Frederick Marx post-1846 when he bought the property.

[102] Model Farms - Planned and model farmsteads were a peculiarly British type, inspired by the agricultural revolution of the late 18th and 19th centuries and were built by and for landed estates, like Arlebury, which played a prominent role in agricultural improvement. The term 'model farm' was not used until the mid-19th century, and it was commonly coined for the farmstead of the 'home farm' closest to the great house of an estate. Many such farmsteads in this period were planned to courtyard layouts, they also advertised the wealth and status of the owner and interest in agricultural innovation. Historic England; Rural Buildings and Landscapes NHPP Activity 4F1 (Pastscape), part of the National Heritage Protection Plan.

[103] The drive was purchased by the Arlebury Park Barns Estate Management Company on behalf of the residents of The Barns in c.2010.

Cottage and Arlebury Park Cottage, and then round into The Barns courtyard.[104][105][106]

Figure 24 - The driveway to The Barns, looking north off the Avenue Photograph September 2015

This is the entrance created to access the relocated farm, probably in about 1862. On the right-hand side of the driveway here, just to the left of this photograph, immediately inside the brick and flint boundary wall is 'Trees', seen in the photograph below).

Figure 25 – 'Trees' Photograph 2015
'Trees' is a pleasing, red brick, late Victorian house. It does not appear in the 1891 census but is shown on the 1896 OS map and included in documents dated c.1899 and may have been where the farm bailiff lived.

Grand entrances

The other very significant changes introduced by the Marx family after 1846 (and again by the Walfords from 1883) were increasingly sweeping, curvaceous drive ways. This was a popular way of displaying property, providing an unfolding vista of a large house in its spacious grounds. The figures below show

---

[104] 'The Barns' (eight houses, six of them grouped round a central courtyard, lie slightly further north east of The Mews, and north of the kitchen gardens and includes 'The Old Bothy', originally a gardeners' cottage or hut.

[105] What Elizabeth Martin calls the 'back drive' from the rear of the house, heading east, is the old farm track between house, the stables and the original farm when located in The Dean. It is shown on both the 1870 OS map and the 1943 survey, page 23.

[106] The 1943 survey - just prior to purchase by the Witchards in 1944 - is also interesting because it shows both the double entrance layout, little if at all changed from the 19th century, and also the land owned by the estate south of The Avenue (Lots 5, 6 and 7).

how this way of displaying the house (and the status of the owners) evolved over the years. The 1846 sketch below shows the relatively modest house approached by a straight, workman-like entrance off The Avenue. By 1870 (Figure 27), there is still a single entrance but it is more curvaceous[107].

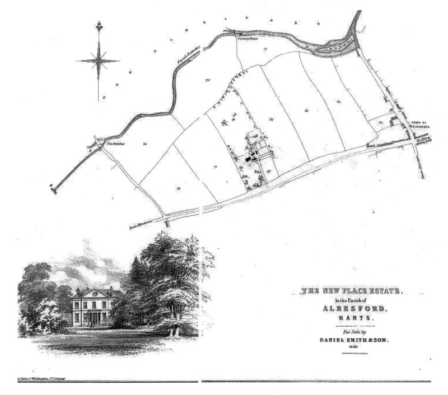

Figure 26 - The 1846 auction sketch with straight entrance
Jervoise of Herriard Collection: Hampshire Record Office:44M69/E22/1/2

By 1870, the single, dead-straight driveway had been given more of a sweep to enhance the approach to the house.

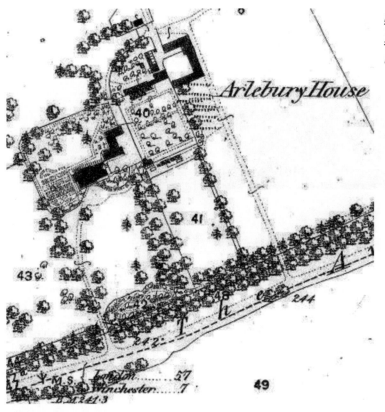

Figure 27 – Detail from the 1870 OS map 25":1 mile
Hampshire Record Office

---

[107] In 2015, some coping on the boundary wall had to be repaired and the specialist stonemason thought this section of wall was laid slightly differently here, perhaps indicating where the original, single entrance had been.

Then, using the 1896 OS map below, when the estate was owned by the Walford family who purchased it in 1883, we can see how Arle Bury had perhaps achieved its apotheosis as a private country house. There were sweeping entrances with lodges to the east and west, the enlarged house had acquired its Italianate Tower, and there were spacious grounds in the parkland or 'designed landscape' style, although the more elaborate parterre to the west of the house, shown in 1870 had gone. Every pleasure and convenience were offered. By this time, as well, the railway had arrived, so commuting between Alresford and the Walford business in Piccadilly was much simplified.

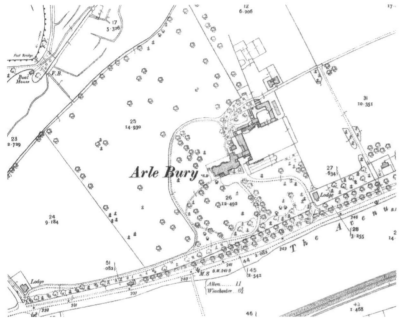

Figure 28 – Detail from 1896 OS map, 42.5, 2nd ed. 25":1 mile
Hampshire Record Office

By now, the elaborate entrances have been further embellished with a looping drive round to the back of the stables and farmery; probably a tradesmen's entrance

Figure 29 - The Gatekeepers' Lodge at the eastern entrance
– Photograph 2019

The 1896 OS map above shows the sweeping drive ways flanked at east and west entrances by lodges. The Martin family bought Arlebury in 1949 before selling back to the Witchards in the mid-1970s but they still own both east and west lodges. In renovating the West Lodge (where Elizabeth Martin lives) in 2015-16, a downpipe was found marked 1894, very possibly when the lodges were built. It has been retained as a souvenir by the front door

Figure 30 - Main entrance looking towards The Avenue Photograph, October 2015

The eastern Gatekeeper's Lodge (Figure 29 above) is just to the left of the main gates, that look out towards The Avenue. The gate piers at the western lodge (now in separate ownership) are identical.

What Arlebury was like by the 20th century

The Walford family bought Arle Bury House and estate in 1883 following the death of George Francis Marx. They may have completed the extension of the house and addition of the tower rather than the Marx family - copying FJP Marx's designs, perhaps - and almost certainly re-designed the driveways (again) and added the two gatekeepers' lodges. By now photography was a fairly usual method of recording things and a number of black & white pictures allow us to take a tour around the exterior of the house.

Figure 31 - Front (south facing) of Arle Bury. Photograph early 1900s

Reproduced by kind permission of Alresford Heritage

Figure 32 - Arle Bury from the west. Photograph early 1900s

Reproduced by kind permission of Alresford Heritage

The large bow window and logia next to it face the western sun. Dr Mary Jones's account of Admiral John Locke Marx's childhood at Arlebury in the 1850s & 1860s refers to *'... its spacious grounds and verandas'*, probably much the same as the logia shown here[108].

Auction details in 1846 didn't include a rear view of the original, smaller property before it was enlarged but the photographs in Figures 33, 34 & 35 show the property much extended in stages after 1846.

Figure 33 – Arle Bury from the north

Reproduced by kind permission of Alresford Heritage[109]

---

[108] A Naval Life: Edited Diaries & Papers of Admiral John Locke Marx 1852-1939. Ed. M Jones, Persona Press, Ch.1.
[109] The name on Figure 33 'C Hunt' is identified by Godfrey Andrews of Alresford Heritage as likely to be Claude Hunt, a well-known local photographer. The similarity of the writing 'Arle Bury' suggests that the photographs in Figures 31 & 32 were also taken by Mr. Hunt.

Note the high screening to the left of the photograph above (Figure 33), which would have shielded the private garden from what were then the domestic offices and stable yard. At this time there is only a simple lawn below the steps from the terrace. It has been suggested that the Walfords may have been 'plant hunters' and could have created a new, more formal garden here to display their botanical trophies[110] but there is nothing here now of an exotic nature. More details on the modern gardens are provided in Part 7 following.

The two much more recent photographs below (c.1990 and 2015 respectively) provide distant views of the house from the north, possibly from a similar point that William Cobbett wrote about in 'Rural Rides' in 1822: *'From Stratton I went on to Northington Down; then round to the South of the Grange Park (Alex. Baring's), down to Abbotson[sic], and over some pretty little green hills to Alresford, which is a nice little town of itself, but which presents a singularly beautiful view from the last little hill coming from Abbotson'[111].* Cobbett didn't specifically mention Arle Bury; a significantly smaller house then but it now dominates the landscape. Mr John Walford thought he had taken his B&W photograph (below left) in the 1990s although this precise view is now sadly much obscured by extensive hedging planted about 2012. The latter view is from a higher viewpoint, north of Drove Lane, where the land rises sharply up to Fob Down and Abbotstone.

Figures 34 & 35 below - Distant views of Arlebury Park House from the north

© Reproduced by kind permission of John Walford, c. 1990 & © Andrew Field, October 2015

---

[110] Although the gardens now contain nothing very exotic, it is mentioned in a Manpower Services commissioned report as including exotic species but they are not named. It is possible that, although in the parkland rather than the garden, this is a reference to specimen trees such as the Cedars of Lebanon, which are non-native.

[111] http://www.gutenberg.org/files/34238/34238-h/34238-h.htm

Part 7- The parkland, garden & wider setting of Arlebury Park House[112]

Sweeps, curves and 'openness' are typical of the English landscape style of gardening, and a 'ha-ha' would keep grazing sheep in the parkland, whilst ensuring unbroken views across the countryside. The lawns might also come right up to the house with less attention to regular flower borders, and specimen trees were much admired. This is a good description of Arlebury to this day. Much farm land had been acquired and then gradually sold from the original estate. The heart of the estate, though, around Arlebury House itself, the Mews and the Barns, with pasture and the river valley to the north and fields to the east and west, remain to this day. They are registered in the official Hampshire list of historic parks & gardens and are part of the Itchen Valley Area of Special Landscape Quality.

Figure 36 - The listed historic park

The diagonally striped area shows the listed area, as does the aerial photo on page 1.[113]

©*Reproduced by kind permission of Winchester City Council*

---

[112] A much more detailed record of the garden and parkland has been provided to the Hampshire Gardens Trust
[113] Based on OS maps and other documents, a case could be made on historic grounds to extend the defined area further east up to The Dean on the edge of the town. This would then include the Recreation Ground and what is called 'Industrial estate' on the map above (currently being redeveloped, mainly for housing as part of Winchester's Local Plan 2011-2031).

Arlebury's parkland & gardens, & countryside heritage

When the land was acquired by William Harris in 1774, the land would have been mainly pasture, with water meadows to the north alongside the river. It is not wholly clear who created the parkland (which is a 'designed landscape', featuring important specimen trees) and the original, formal garden to the west of the house. A well-stocked kitchen garden for fruit and vegetables, though, is likely to have been an important part of the layout from the start.

We know that William Harris sold the property in 1812 to Richard Bailey, who sold in 1814 to John Rawlinson and an 'early nineteenth century document'[114] cites '... melon ground, pleasure grounds, plantations and gardens'. More definitively, after Mr Rawlinson died, the 1846 auction notice[115] lists 'well planted grounds, having an important frontage upon the highroad, from which it is screened by ornamental plantations'. The same documents, under the heading 'The Kitchen Garden' say '... enclosed by Fruit Walls, with Melon-Ground, outer Slips, Horse-Paddock, &c.'

Appendix II in 'Hampshire's Countryside Heritage: Volume 5 Historic Parks and Gardens, provides what is called a 'Preliminary list of Historic Parks & Gardens in Hampshire, recorded in a Manpower Services Commission sponsored project (mainly concerned with jobs for unemployed people). It notes 'New Place built 1780 – 1790 by William Harris' and specifies 'formal gardens'. The type of site is codified GPFIFTNE: G – Garden landscape, P – Park landscape, F – Formal layout, IF – Informal layout, T – Trees, N – Native species and E – Exotic species.

The 1870 OS map indicates that the formal garden lay west of the house (see page 36) but it is not shown on the later 1896 version. The new garden seems to have been created some time after the early 1900s by the Walfords (see old B&W photographs, page 39) and remains here today, merging with the rising downs beyond, across the river, to Fob Down.

**Figure 37 - Formal gardens from 1st floor of house, looking north to the downs**
© _Photograph September 2015_
The border in the middle of the photo, beyond the sun dial, marks an old ha-ha.

---

[114] Undated and source unascribed. One of several articles by R Elliot in Alresford Parish Magazine in 1980s
[115] HRO 44M69/E22/1/2

The sun dial makes a good feature in the garden, standing just over 6 feet high.

Figure 39 Looking west from the lower garden ©*Photograph September 2015*

The western gable end of the house is to the left of the photograph here. The hedge marks the approximate site of the original formal gardens, which were significantly bigger, before being relocated to the north of the house, where they have the advantage of providing views over the valley to the rising chalk hills (see Figure 37).

The veteran trees at Arlebury

What is now the formal garden, just north of the house and shown in the series of photographs above, is modest but the parkland (or 'designed landscape', a style belonging to the period c. 1720 – 1820[116]) is remarkable both for the ways it opens up views across the valley to the north and for its huge, veteran specimen trees[117]. They include magnificent lime trees (as in The Avenue, immediately south of the house), and several huge Cedars of Lebanon. The latter, exotic introductions, were a favourite of

---

[116] Roy Stone in 'Landscapes Through the Ages 1420-1940'. Conran, Octopus 1992
[117] The veteran trees are protected by a Tree Preservation Order taken out by the residents in 2014 as part of the process of protecting the area from development. In 2015, a Holm Oak (evergreen oak) 2115T4 was felled by emergency application to Winchester City Council after storm damage threatened to break a fence, block the driveway and allow sheep in the field to escape. See also Cedar of Lebanon below.

Capability Brown (b.1716, d. 1783). His ideas - sweeping away formality with curvaceous driveways and vistas of great trees - were widely copied. The Woodland Trust records that grand cedars were planted in parks and large gardens, and widely used in the 18th century as '... *the accessory for every stately home and mansion from 1740s onwards'*.

Figure 40 – Cedar of Lebanon at the front of the house – *Photograph September 2015*
Sadly, this splendid example had to be felled, badly diseased and in danger of shedding its great limbs, in November 2018. The tree surgeons reckoned it might be about 170 years old, so this suggests it was planted by John Rawlinson or Francis Marx, who bought the property in 1846 and set about the aggrandisement of his estate.

Figure 41 - Sweet Chestnut to the west of the formal garden - ©*Photograph September 2015*

In addition to cedars there are limes, a walnut, magnolia, the sweet chestnut (in the photograph shown here), a paulownia (foxglove tree), acers and English oaks: a mix of native, naturalized and the more exotic! Inevitably, they will decay with time and fierce autumn and winter gales can cause great damage, so new trees such as a sapling English oak and a hawthorn have recently been planted too, a policy that will be continued

The ancient heronry

The cedars are also the site of an ancient heronry. The herons stand, sentinel-like, on the flat tops of the trees.

A reminder of the sheep fairs

Sheep have long been an important part of Alresford, with sheep fairs stretching back over the centuries and drove lanes converging on the town. To this day, helping to keep alive the 'spirit of the place', there is a small but pleasant reminder of this at Arlebury Park House, within half a mile of the town centre's Broad Street, where the livestock markets were held[118]. Front and back of the house, the small fields purchased by Arlebury Parkland Ltd in 2015 to be kept specifically as pasture land (see Foreword), are still grazed. The breed of sheep varies: curly-horned Portlands, black Welsh Mountain and cross-bred mule sheep. These pastures (about 6 acres in total) and surrounding fields to the north and west, are possibly ancient meadow land, classified by Natural England as MG5, meaning unimproved grass that has not been artificially fertilised or ploughed for generations; only about 6000 ha. of this type of meadowland still exist in England.

The wider setting

The wider setting of the house – beyond the parklands - also adds greatly to its heritage value. The House, Mews and Barns are bounded on the southern edge by a handsome flint wall with brick piers and coping that probably dates from the early 19th century and runs the whole length of The Avenue. The road heads eastwards to the town centre and thence towards Alton, and westwards towards Winchester, some 8 miles distant.

In 1753 an Act of Parliament permitted the building of the turnpike. Tolls collected were partially reimbursed to shareholders in Turnpike Trusts and partially used for the maintenance and refurbishment of the 19 miles of road from Winchester to Alton. The current Toll House (also locally called the 'Round

---

[118] Some 800 years since they first began, a street market is still held weekly in Broad Street, on Thursdays, operated by the Town Trust. Plants, eggs, vegetables ... but no sheep or cattle these days.

House') dates from the mid-19th century and was part of the Arlebury estate, which is just to the left of the photograph below. It is marked on the various sketches and maps, included as Lot 4 in the 1944 sale (page 23).

Figure 43- The Toll House (Grade II listed) on the old turnpike, c. 1900
Reproduced by kind permission of Alresford Heritage

Winchester City Council's landscape and historic environment appraisals[119] identified the following characteristics of this area, including the *'distinctive lime avenue'* that, together with the landmark of Arlebury Park House and the river valley, create a *'sense of place'*. This is described as a *'highly sensitive area; any development would severely impact on biodiversity, landscape and heritage character. The Arle/Itchen valley floor is dominated by permanent pasture, semi- or unimproved grassland with historic water meadows and species associated with wetland areas'.*

There is no complete record of the flora and fauna in the parkland, part of the Itchen Valley Area of Special Landscape Quality and close to protected SAC and SSSI habitats. The range of wild animals, birds and reptiles (including species protected under European legislation and the Wildlife & Countryside Act) is wide ranging but requires expert input to do it justice. There is widespread concern about damage to rare chalk streams such as the Upper Itchen and Arle, where wildlife is declining, probably due to water pollution which damages the food chain. The following, though, have been reported by knowledgeable local residents:

- Field mice, possibly dormice, yellow-necked and wood mice, possibly harvest mice; field voles, possibly bank and water voles
- Slow worms, grass snakes, toads and frogs
- Hedgehogs, bats, squirrels (grey) and occasional Roe deer
- Waterfowl, including egrets, swans, Canada geese, mallards, etc.
- Herons, green woodpecker, lesser spotted woodpecker, owls
- Bumble bees and honey bees, mortar bees; Red Admiral, Peacock, Brimstone butterflies.

---

[119] Winchester City Council Local Plan Part 2 Landscape & Historic Environment Appraisals

On the northern edge of the park is the Arle river walk, part of the 2000 Millennium Trail. North of the river, the land rises to the Hampshire Downs; Abbotstone is to the north-west and Old Alresford to the north-east. All are favourite walks for local people and visitors and provide views admired by William Cobbett nearly two hundred years earlier, in his Rural Rides 1822.

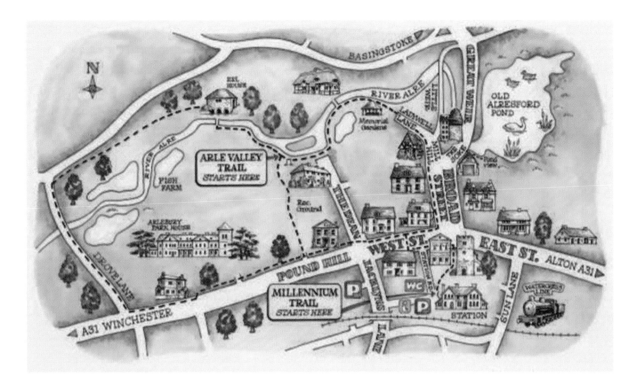

Figure 44 - The stylised map of the town and Millennium Trail
© *Reproduced by kind permission of New Alresford Town Council*

Part 8 - A final note on historical loss of power and influence

Over the centuries, county families such as the successive owners of Arlebury lost social, economic and political influence both locally and on a wider front. Political power, embodied in the right to vote, was extremely limited and local people (tenants, employees, and local tradesmen) would be disinclined to vote against a preferred candidate who was supported by the landowner. In her novel *'Wives and Daughters'*, written about a time before the passing of the Reform Bill, Elizabeth Gaskell wrote '... *every man-jack gave his vote to the liege lord...'* and *'This was no unusual instance of the influence of the great landowners over humbler neighbours in those days ...'* The third Reform Act (1885) meant that £10 (in annual rent or land value) secured males the vote. It had been £200 in William Harris's day, a hundred years earlier.

The Representation of the People Act 1918, gave the vote to all men, and to women over 30 who met certain property qualifications. In 1928 the Representation of the People (Equal Franchise) Act gave the vote to all women over the age of 21 on equal terms with men, so power was no longer so concentrated in the hands of a few.

The fate of many country houses and their owners

The agricultural depressions in the late 1800s and early 1900s, with cheaper imports from abroad, had made estates much less profitable. Local political power and status were reduced when county councils were created in 1888 and parish councils in 1895. The two World Wars and Great Depression all contributed to the loss of a swathe of Britain's historical families and architectural heritage. Arlebury was never an aristocratic estate but even relatively modest ones such as this would now be too costly to maintain, especially if there was also upkeep of a London property as well, which both the Marx and Walford families owned. Staff to run them was much more difficult to find, wages were rising, and taxation to pay war debts was ever increasing (both on income and on inherited wealth, the dreaded 'Death Duties'). So, houses like Arlebury and their ownership by once powerful local families became increasingly irrelevant when compared to their influence in preceding centuries. The 'Big House' at Arlebury had been a bedrock of rural society, supporting local employment and patronage: what would have been considered then 'the natural order'. This had now changed and as grand houses were lost or radically altered, so their histories have often been lost.

Tracing family histories on the internet is vastly increasing the amount of information that is available now, although it is usually for personal and immediate family interest, and may never form part of a public record. It is noticeable that the Hampshire Record Office and local churches in New Alresford and Tichborne contain numerous references to the dominant families at Arlebury as a private residence: the Harris family from around 1774, the Marx family from 1846 and the Walfords from 1883 until the 1940s. The records though are sparser once we enter the post-war period, when the Witchard and Martin families owned the estate, so I am grateful for the personal reminiscences that Jim Witchard and Elizabeth Martin have afforded.

Legislation & the built heritage

Saving the country's built heritage has been helped by successive Ancient Monuments Protection Acts from the 1880s and the Town & Country Planning Acts, 1944 to 1968. They gradually tightened restrictions on what could be done to old buildings, although they were often not enforced either by local authorities or public opinion. The 1968 Act began to slow demolitions noticeably, requiring owners to wait for permission to demolish a building, rather than simply notifying the local authority. The authorities could also issue a 'Building Preservation Notice', effectively giving listed building status.

At least as important, though, has been a change in public opinion. Alongside an interest in family histories, people began to recognise that these properties and their settings, often areas of outstanding landscape quality in themselves, and the histories of their owners, were of value for the future as much as the past.

THE END … FOR NOW, AT LEAST!

Appendices

Appendix 1 - Hampshire & Isle of Wight Wildlife Trust 'Living Landscape'
Reproduced by kind permission HIWWT

The Arlebury estate is just below the word 'Fobdown' on the map below. Although land was owned on both sides of the river in the past, the remaining estate is solely to the south of it.

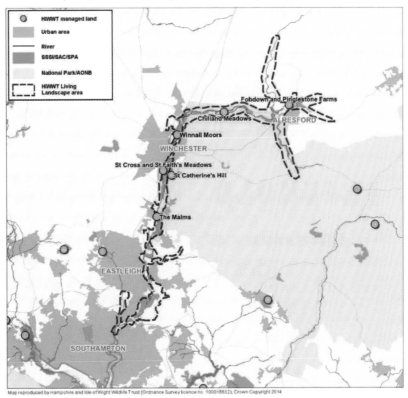

Appendix 2 - Jane Austen; any links with Arlebury?

Given the inter-connectiveness of members of 'the gentry' in the early 19th century, it is inevitable that the many fans of Jane Austen will ask if there were any links between her, or her family, and the Harris family, living just 11 or 12 miles away. They may have been acquaintances but seemingly little more. Jane Austen was born in 1775, the year after William Harris acquired the site for New Place, so he was already nearly 40 by then although, coincidentally, both died in 1817. Jane Austen moved to Chawton Cottage in 1809 and would frequently have visited her brother at Chawton House or attended local social events where the families could have met. Even though William Harris sold the estate in 1812, the whole family was buried in St John's Church in Alresford so they presumably continued to live in the area and so their lives 'overlapped', albeit only by about 8 years. Decisively, though, there seems to be no mention of such a friendship in Deirdre Le Faye's comprehensive review of Jane Austen's letters[120]. Nor is there any mention of Richard Bailey who bought the estate in 1812 or the subsequent owner, from 1814, John Rawlinson, when the property was still called 'New Place'.

---

[120] Deirdre Le Faye wrote the definitive factual biography, *Jane Austen: A Family Record*, plus a new edition of *Jane Austen's Letters*, several other books, and numerous scholarly articles.

HAMPSHIRE.

THE

ESTATE OF NEW PLACE,

WITH ITS

MANSION & FAMOUS TROUT FISHERY,

CLOSE TO

ALRESFORD,

About Six Miles from WINCHESTER and Eighteen from SOUTHAMTON.

PARTICULARS

OF THE ABOVE VALUABLE

FREEHOLD PROPERTY,

COMPRISING THE

Mansion of New Place,

THE PROMINENT FEATURE AMIDST THE PICTURESQUE SCENERY ON APPROACHING
THE TOWN OF ALRESFORD FROM WINCHESTER,

SURROUNDED BY WELL-PLANTED GROUNDS,

HAVING AN EXTENSIVE AND IMPORTANT FRONTAGE UPON THE HIGH ROAD,

FROM WHICH IT IS

SCREENED BY ORNAMENTAL PLANTATIONS;

TOGETHER WITH

AN ESTATE,

IN A MOST PERFECT AND COMPACT RING FENCE,

OF

ABOUT 105 ACRES,

PART

VERY VALUABLE WATER MEADOWS,

Extending to and embracing the RIVER, which bounds it on the lower or North Side for about a Mile, affording
some of the

BEST TROUT FISHING IN THE COUNTY,

Which will be sold by Auction, by

Messrs. DANIEL SMITH & SON,

AT THE MART, NEAR THE BANK OF ENGLAND,

On FRIDAY, 18th Day of SEPTEMBER, 1846,

(Unless an acceptable Offer shall be previously made by Private Contract.)

It may be viewed with Cards, which, with Particulars and Lithographic Plans, may be had at Messrs. JACOB and
JOHNSON's Library, Winchester; at the Hotels, Southampton; at the Auction Mart; of Messrs. DUNN, HOPKINS,
and CARTER, Solicitors, Alresford; and of Messrs. DANIEL SMITH & SON, Land Agents, in Waterloo-place,
Pall-mall, and Windsor.

PARTICULARS

THE DESIRABLE

ESTATE OF NEW PLACE

is pleasantly situated in a highly picturesque and healthy part of the County of Hants,

CLOSE TO

THE TOWN OF ALRESFORD,

on its entrance from *WINCHESTER*, which with its Railway Station is only about Six Miles distant, bringing it within Two and a half Hours' Journey of London.

It is surrounded by a Neighbourhood of the highest respectability, and a famous Sporting Country, being in the Centre of the H. Hunt, and only Eighteen Miles from Southampton.

THE PROPERTY CONSISTS OF A

MODERATE SIZED MANSION,

with good Stabling, &c. and a remarkably

COMPACT AND VALUABLE FARM,

OF

Superior Arable, Pasture, and Water Meadow Land,

Bounded by the RIVER for nearly a Mile.

THE HOUSE

stands on the higher part of the Estate at a short pleasant distance but perfectly screened, from the high Road by ornamental Plantations.

It has an important Frontage *extending to the Town*, rendering a considerable portion of the Lands very

ELIGIBLE FOR BUILDING,

the Fields sloping to the River and commanding the romantic Scenery of its opposite Bank.

THE ESTATE IS FREEHOLD,

except the FISHERY, which is held on Three Lives by Copy of Court-Roll under the Bishop of Winchester, subject to an annual Quit-rent of **£6.**

The House is substantially built, with strong slated Roof, and has two Fronts.

IT CONTAINS

On the UPPER FLOOR,

Four large Attic Bed-Rooms, a smaller ditto, and Linen-Closet, with large Landing. &c.

On the FIRST FLOOR,

Six family Bed-Rooms and a Dressing-Room, a spacious Landing, Water-closet; Housemaid's ditto, with Water laid on, Sink, &c.; Principal and Back Staircases;

The GROUND FLOOR

Comprises an *ENTRANCE-HALL*, 16 Feet by 12 Feet;

A DRAWING-ROOM, with Bow, 21 Feet 6 Inches by 21 Feet;

A DINING-ROOM, 22 Ft. by 18; a Library, 21 Ft. by 19; a Breakfast-Room, 17 Ft. by 16; and a Gentleman's Dressing-Room, all about 12 Feet high.

THE DOMESTIC OFFICES

consist of Servants' Hall, Housekeeper's Room, Butler's Pantry, Men-Servants' Bed-Room, Larder, Pantry, &c. with good Wine and Beer Cellars.

ON THE EAST SIDE

is a large *Court-Yard* with a *Brewhouse* and Laundry; *double Coach-House* and Granary; Two THREE-STALLED STABLES and *Saddle-Room*, with Groom's Room above; another Stable for Four Horses; Cow-House, Piggery, Wood-Shed, and Workshop; adjoining is

THE KITCHEN GARDEN,

enclosed by Fruit Walls, with Melon-Ground, outer Slips, Horse-Paddock, &c.

There are Two Pews in the Parish Church of ALRESFORD, *from which the Mansion is distant about a quarter of a mile.*

John Rawlinson Esq., owner of New Place 1814 -1846, is listed as the proprietor as immediately below.

64	**Paddock**	69	**The Lawn**	75	**River**
65	**Upper Brook Field**	70	**Hither Nineteen Acres**	76	**Upper Common**
66	**Middle Brook Field**	71	**Further Nineteen Acres**	77	**River**
66	**Lower Brook Field**	72	**Lower Common**	78	**Island**
67	**Paddock**	73	**River**		
68	**Mansion & buildings**	74	**Middle Common**		

Although recognisably the same, a few of the numbers and names used for the sale lots following John Rawlinson's death in 1846 when the property was sold to Francis Marx are slightly different.

Appendix 4a
'Sale lots at the auction [1846] of the 'New Place Estate' with its mansion, trout fishery and 105 acres of land close to Alresford, County of Southampton.'

Lot		State	Acres	Roods	Perches	Further notes
69	Site of Mansion, Buildings, Pleasure Grounds, Garden		4	1	25	This was Upper & Lower Stokes Close sold by Robert Boyes to Wm. Harris (founder of Arlebury) in c. 1774. By 1846, the sale lots included the further acreages listed.
68	Garden Paddock	Pasture	1	0	15	SE of stable yard by house, stretching south to the highway
70	The Lawn	Pasture	6	1	38	Front & back of mansion: north to water meadow (75) & south to the highway
67	Lower Brook Furlong	Arable	12	3	5	Rectangular field to east of mansion: north to water meadows (77 & 75) & south to highway
66	Middle Brook Furlong	Arable	14	1	11	Rectangular field east of Lower Brook Furlong (67): north to water meadows (77 & 75) & south to highway
65	Upper Brook Furlong	Arable	10	2	38	Rectangular field east of Middle Brook Furlong (66) to edge of town: north to river and island (79) & south to highway
64	Dean Paddock	Pasture	1	0	6	*'In No.64 adjoining the Town is a Spacious Farm-yard, two large barns, Cattle-sheds, &c., and there is a Brick and Tiled Fishing House in the Meadows'*
77	Upper Mead	Water Meadow	5	0	11	Between fields 67, 66, 65 and river
75	Middle Mead	Water Meadow	12	3	30	Between lawn (70) and river
73	Lower Mead	Water Meadow	10	1	6	Between field 72 and river
71	Hither Nineteen Acres	Arable	11	1	14	Rectangular field to west of mansion: north to water meadows 73 & 75 & south to highway

---

[121] 1843 Tithe Map Hampshire Record Office 21M65/F7/167/2

72	Hither Nineteen Acres	Arable	10	1	18	Field to west of 71 north to water meadow 73 & south to highway.
74	Part of the River	Water	0	3	10	Trout fishing
76	Part of the River	Water	1	0	20	Trout fishing
78	Part of the River	Water	2	1	33	Trout fishing
79	The Island	Sedge Plat	0	2	25	May mean 'sedge plants', typical wetland plants
Total			105	3	25	

We still speak of 'acres' (or 4 Roods) but these other area and length measurements were little used in England after the beginning of the 20th century.

Appendix 5 - Death Certificate for FJP Marx

'Thrown from his horse on Dec 7th when he sustained severe injury of the spine probably fracture from which he died on December 11th 1876. Inquest 13 December 1876'. Hampshire Record Office:20M98/A1

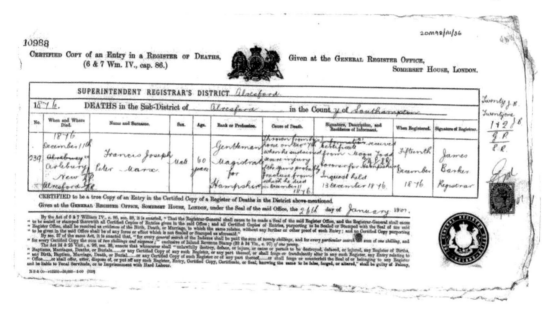

The Reading Mercury for Saturday, 16th December, recorded: *'Fatal Accident in the Hunting Field. Major Marx, who recently met with an accident while hunting, died at Arle Bury, Alresford, on Monday night. Deceased took a great interest in the volunteer movement, and was highly respected in Hampshire.'*

Appendix 6 – An explanation of the sale of estate by William Harris to Richard Bailey 1812

'Release and covenant to levy fine to bar dower of freehold or covenant to surrender copyhold estate called New Place estate', explained by David Rymill, Archivist at Hampshire Record Office, 11M52/413.
This deed, dated October 1812, when William Harris sold to Richard Bailey, sets out in a single document all the things that were supposed to be happening to achieve the sale of the Arlebury property (then still called 'New Place'), some freehold and some copyhold (i.e. subject to the jurisdiction of a Lord of the Manor, possibly the diocese) and, therefore, having to be dealt with separately.

a. The freehold land is principally dealt with by the release. A release is the second part of a two-stage process carried out over two days, known as a 'lease and release': the vendor grants the purchaser a one-year lease of the property one day, and on the next day releases his right to have it back after the year is up. The two documents together make up essentially an outright conveyance and indeed it was the most common form of conveyance for about 200 years.

b. In this case there is an additional element in that there is an undertaking to go through the process of a collusive legal process known as a fine (or 'final concord') in order to get round the possibility of the vendor's wife claiming dower rights if she were subsequently widowed.

c. The formal process by which copyhold land was sold was that the vendor surrendered it into the hands of the Lord of the Manor (acting through a steward, often a local solicitor), and the Lord then admitted the purchaser as the new tenant. By this date the process had become something of a formality, in that the record of the surrender would make it clear who the Lord was supposed to be admitting as the new tenant, subject to the payment of the appropriate entry 'fine' (not a fine in the sense of a penalty, and quite different from the use of the word fine as in final concord above!) In this case, as both freehold and copyhold lands were being dealt with, it gave the purchaser additional security if an obligation on the vendor's part to go through with the surrender process was written into the conveyance of the freehold portion.

Appendix 7
In memory of the Marx family – memorial plaques in St Andrew's Church, Tichborne

Strong links between the Marx family and Tichborne are clearly demonstrated in memorial plaques on the west wall of St Andrew's, either side of the aisle.

*   To the left they record Henrietta Marx [d.1882], daughter of George Marx.
*   The second is 'In pious memory of George Marx [d.1835] and of Selina his wife [d. 1826]' and then lists four children. The second wife of George Marx, Mrs Johnston, is not recorded.
*   The third plaque reads 'In memory of Francis JP Marx of Arle- Bury, Hants Esq., JP son of George Marx b. 1816, d. December 1876'.
*   To the right of the aisle, a fourth memorial reads 'In this church yard lie the earthly remains of A M Selina wife of Francis Marx of Arlebury Hants & daughter of Wadham Locke MP' b.1807 d.1873 at Arlebury. In the church yard, east of the church, there is a stone simply engraved 'Entrance to the vault of F Marx Esq
*   A fifth memorial says 'In loving memory of George Francis Marx of Arle Bury, Hants Esq, JP, late Capt. 68th Durham Light Infantry, son of Francis & Selina Marx b.1849 d.1883.'
*   Mr AH Wood is mentioned in the fifth memorial 'In loving memory of Constance Catherine Jervoise Widow of George Francis Marx Wife of Arthur Hardy Wood b. 1852 d.1916.' She is said to have worn herself out tending wounded WWI patients. It is possible she worked at one of the several thousand auxiliary hospitals set up to cater for the hundreds of thousands of wounded men returning from WWI, either Bishops Court Hospital, Bishops Sutton near Alresford or at Alresford Place Hospital, Old Alresford.

Appendix 8
A very brief note on interior features at Arlebury

There is very little that I can say about the interior layout and features of the house. The interior of the original Georgian house was perhaps left largely untouched until the second pediment and tower were added during the 19th century, greatly extending the property. The thickness (3 feet) of what is now an *internal* wall running front to back of the house, just to the right of the main entrance (itself re-sited from the original property), suggests that it was originally an exterior wall. It includes a coloured glass panel about 5 feet square that would once have sat over a door to the outside. The conversion of the interior to flats in the 20th century was dramatic and destroyed much of the internal layout. Some features of the interior remain though: internal window shutters, wood paneling, fire places, surrounds, cupboards, plaster work, door frames, a massive built-in safe in one of the basement flats, and more – many of which probably date back to the original house.